THE RISE OF THE LIONESSES

To my team, QPR, who made me fall in love with football and to everyone who fought against the odds to make women's football what it is today.

F.L.H.

First published 2023 by Walker Books Ltd
87 Vauxhall Walk, London SE11 5HJ

2 4 6 8 10 9 7 5 3 1

Text © 2023 Florence Lloyd-Hughes

Cover and interior illustrations © 2023 Dan Leydon

The right of Florence Lloyd-Hughes to be identified as author of this work has been asserted in accordance with the Copyright, Designs and Patents Act 1988

This book has been typeset in Century Schoolbook, Tw Cen MT and Bintang

Printed and bound by CPI Group (UK) Ltd, Croydon CR0 4YY

All rights reserved. No part of this book may be reproduced, transmitted or stored in an information retrieval system in any form or by any means, graphic, electronic or mechanical, including photocopying, taping and recording, without prior written permission from the publisher.

British Library Cataloguing in Publication Data: a catalogue record for this book is available from the British Library

ISBN 978-1-5295-1674-6

www.walker.co.uk

THE RISE OF THE LIONESSES

INCREDIBLE MOMENTS — FROM — WOMEN'S FOOTBALL

FLO LLOYD-HUGHES

WALKER BOOKS

CONTENTS

INTRODUCING WOMEN'S FOOTBALL	**6**

EARLY LIONESSES

"IF MEN CAN PLAY FOOTBALL, SO CAN WOMEN": NETTIE HONEYBALL KICKS OFF	11
LEGENDARY LADIES: DICK, KERR LADIES AND LILY PARR	18
CHANGING ENGLAND: GILL COULTARD AND THE DONCASTER BELLES	25
CHANGING THE WORLD: THE USA'S MIA HAMM AND THE '99ERS	34

LEGENDARY LIONESSES

THE INVINCIBLES: ARSENAL'S WINNERS RACHEL YANKEY AND KELLY SMITH	44
FROM CUBS TO LIONESSES: GAME-CHANGING COACH HOPE POWELL	53
GOING FOR GOLD: TEAM GB AT THE LONDON 2012 OLYMPICS	62
BRILLIANT BRONZE: FARA WILLIAMS AND THE FIFA WOMEN'S WORLD CUP 2015	71
STANDING UP AND SPEAKING OUT: ENI ALUKO AND ENGLAND'S NEW DIRECTION	80
GOLDEN TOUCH: LUCY BRONZE AND THE FIFA WOMEN'S WORLD CUP 2019	87

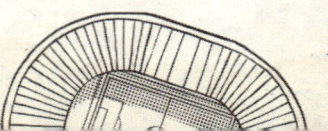

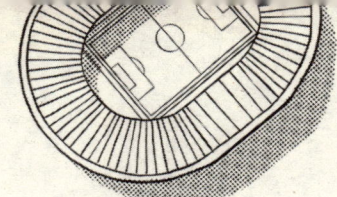

PENALTY PAIN: STEPH HOUGHTON AND THE FIFA WOMEN'S WORLD CUP 2019 — 94

TRIUMPHANT LIONESSES

THE UEFA WOMEN'S EURO 2022: TOURNAMENT OVERVIEW — 105

COACH WITH A PLAN: SARINA WIEGMAN — 109

GOLDEN GIRL: BETH MEAD — 117

THE GIRL WHO BEAT THE BOYS: ELLEN WHITE — 124

EXTRA-TIME EXCELLENCE: GEORGIA STANWAY — 131

THE BACKHEEL THAT STUNNED THE WORLD: ALESSIA RUSSO — 140

THE MOMENT THAT STOPPED THE NATION: CHLOE KELLY — 148

SUPER SUB'S LAST HURRAH: JILL SCOTT — 158

THE CAPTAIN WHO BROUGHT FOOTBALL HOME: LEAH WILLIAMSON — 166

LIONESSES ON THE BALL

ENGLAND DEFEAT WORLD CHAMPIONS: 2022 ENGLAND VERSUS THE USA FRIENDLY — 175

THE FIFA WOMEN'S WORLD CUP 2023: KEY LIONESSES AND THEIR OPPONENTS — 182

INTRODUCING WOMEN'S FOOTBALL

My name is Flo and I'm a football journalist. That means I get to watch football games all over the country and then write and talk about them afterwards. I love football and I'm especially passionate about the women's game. I played loads when I was younger and still sometimes as an adult, and I've seen the women's game change in front of my eyes.

When I was growing up, I was one of the few girls in my school who played, but now girls fill up pitches all over the UK. And it's not just on the pitch where the women's game is becoming more noticeable: there are now former women's players working as presenters on TV and pundits on massive programmes such as "Match of the Day". Women's football has changed from a sport that didn't get the recognition it deserved to one that sells out stadiums and is on the front page of all the national newspapers.

When the England Lionesses beat Germany in the final of the UEFA Women's Euro 2022, their victory capped one of the most unforgettable summers in English football and one that will go down in sporting history. It was the first time since 1966, when the men's team won the World Cup, that England had won a major tournament. Nearly 90,000 people were cheering in the stands at Wembley and millions were watching at home. I was lucky enough to be there and I screamed when the final whistle blew, because I knew that this was going to be a day that would change women's football in England for ever.

Watching that game inspired me to look back at the history of the Lionesses. I wanted to learn more about the early days of women's football and understand how the Lionesses had become the top squad they are today. I decided to write a book and share what I found out. Whether you are an old or new football fan, I want you to be inspired by the rise of the Lionesses and be as excited about the future of the women's game as I am.

Women's football hasn't always been popular in England and the Lionesses' success didn't happen overnight. Generations of women have overcome massive challenges so girls today can play the game they love. The success of the Lionesses goes all the way back to the tenacity of teams such as Dick, Kerr Ladies and the Doncaster Belles, who played on despite a ban by the Football Association (FA) that lasted decades. While there is still a long way to go before women's and men's football are treated completely equally, attitudes are slowly changing. Captain of the 2022 Euros team, Leah Williamson, was immediately made an OBE (Officer of the Order of the British Empire) in recognition of her services to women's football and three of her teammates, including Beth Mead, were made MBEs (Members of the Order of the British Empire). This is something that players of previous generations could never have imagined, given that the FA once ruled that football was "unsuitable for females".

I've chosen what I think are the most important stories in the history of the Lionesses. I'm going to tell you all about the players from that victorious 2022 Euros squad, such as Chloe Kelly and Jill Scott, and also trailblazing women you might never have heard of. These include Nettie Honeyball and Lily Parr, who defied society to play the game, the vibrant USA World Cup squad, known as "The '99ers", who changed the global game and player-turned-coach Hope Powell, who fought for her squad. I've also looked at the FIFA Women's World Cup 2023 and showcased the superstar players that fans should keep their eyes on.

It's been amazing to relive some of the Lionesses' most memorable games and tournaments, and highlight so many other special moments, some of which I've been lucky enough to cover as a journalist, and others that I've just read about in history books. I hope you enjoy reading these stories too and finding out more about these incredible moments in women's football.

Flo Lloyd-Hughes

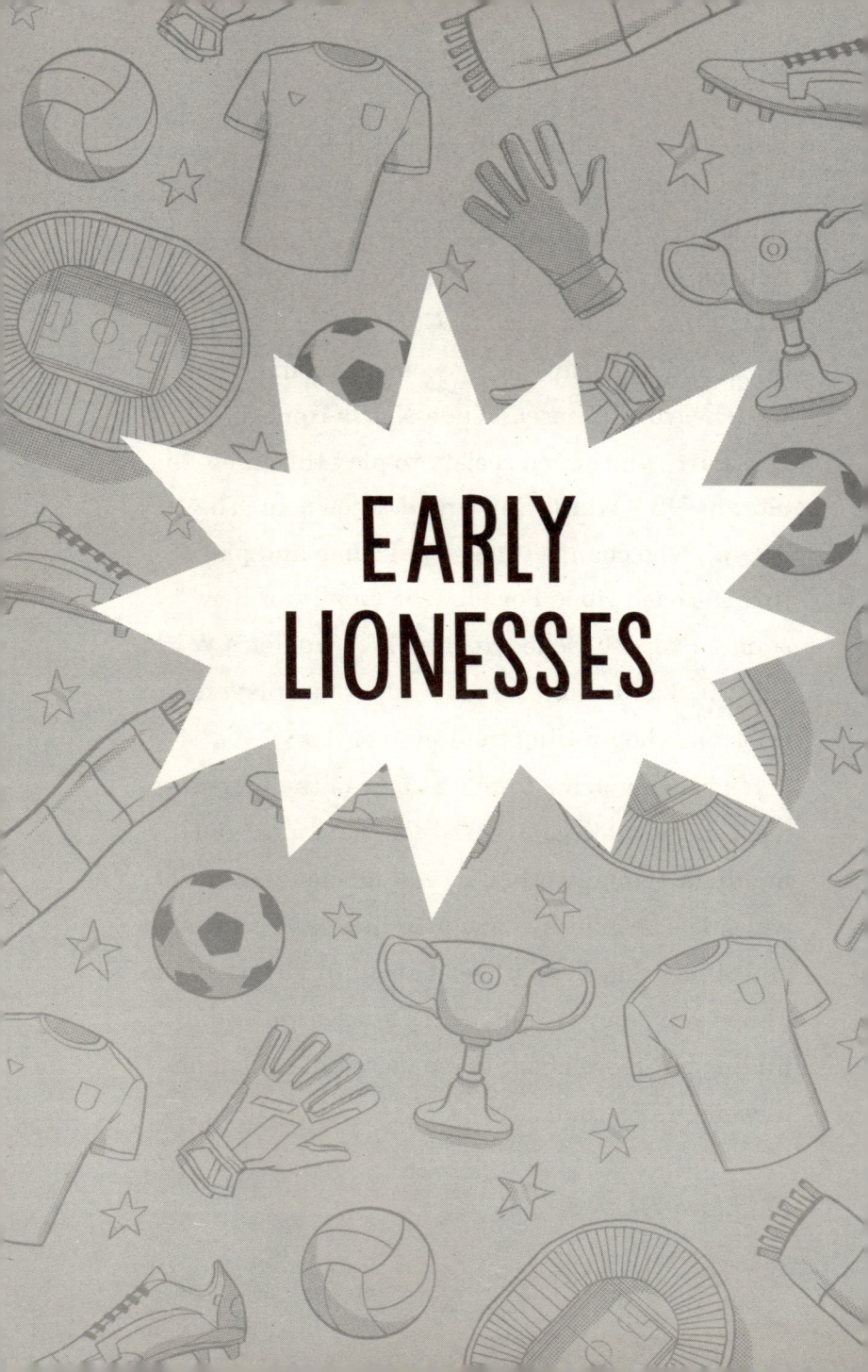

EARLY LIONESSES

"IF MEN CAN PLAY FOOTBALL, SO CAN WOMEN": NETTIE HONEYBALL KICKS OFF

In July 2022, over 80,000 people packed into a sold-out Wembley stadium to watch England take on Germany in the 2022 Euros final. It was a historic moment for women's football in England. That summer, we were glued to our TV screens as women's football took the country by storm. But not many people know that this wasn't the first time that women's football had gripped the nation. Around a hundred years ago, women's football was drawing huge crowds up and down the country.

Women have played football in England for hundreds of years. From poems, we know that women were involved in the game as far back as the 1600s. In the 1700s, fisherwomen in Scotland played informal games with each other. But it wasn't until the 1800s, when football was formally established as a sport, with written rules and regulations, that the women's game really spread.

> ### FOOTBALL FACT
> The first set of official rules for football were written down in 1848 by students at Cambridge, who wanted to make the differences between football and rugby clear. The Laws of the Game were drawn up in 1863 and are still used today.

Once there were proper rules, clubs and teams could play each other without arguments. Men's leagues started up and, by the late 1800s, women's teams were forming up and down the country too. At the time, it wasn't normal for women to play sport. Women didn't have much independence and weren't allowed to vote. They were expected to be at home to cook, clean and look after their children. But, despite this, women were playing football anyway.

The first officially recorded women's football match took place in 1881 between two teams, one representing Scotland and one England. Neither team were actually representing their country, as the match had been organized by two theatre businessmen as a way to make money.

Alec Gordon, from Scotland, had seen how popular the sport was getting across Britain and the potential money that could be made from organizing a series of matches. He decided to partner with another businessman from England and put on games in Scotland and England. Most of the players involved weren't even footballers, but were women from a ballet company.

It's hard to know how many informal matches were actually played before this game in 1881. At this time, newspapers were regularly writing about the men's game, but rarely reported on women's football.

When the women's game *was* written about by male journalists, the tone was disrespectful and rude. The coverage focused on the players' appearance, not the actual match. Journalists would stress that football was a game for men and it was about physical strength. There were even violent pitch invasions at some of the women's games, where spectators ran onto the pitch to disrupt the match.

This didn't deter keen women players. In 1894, the British Ladies' Football Club (BLFC), the most famous team of the time, was founded. The team was set up by Lady Florence Dixie, a wealthy aristocrat. As a feminist, she believed that men and women should be treated equally in all areas of society.

Lady Florence sponsored the team. Alfred Hewitt Smith was the manager, and the captain was a woman called Nettie Honeyball. This was a made-up name and we still don't know her real name, but some historians think it was Mary Hutson. At the time, lots of women were scared about what might happen if they were seen to be doing things that were considered "unladylike". Football was one of those things, so it seems likely that Nettie came up with a fake name to protect herself.

Nettie needed players for her new team so she posted an advert in the newspaper. When she was interviewed by a newspaper in 1895, she said the aim of her team was to show the world "that women are not the 'ornamental and useless' creatures men have pictured". In another interview in the same year, she insisted that "if men can play football, so can women".

Despite her passion and commitment, lots of people laughed at Nettie's team. Some even said that it was dangerous for women to play because there was a myth that it would damage their bodies. Others were outraged that Nettie was going to charge for tickets to the team's games and at the idea that women could make money from sport.

Most of the discussion was about what the women would wear to play. At this time, women wore corsets around their waists that were very uncomfortable and restrictive, and were expected to cover their legs and ankles. This clothing was not easy to play football in. But Nettie and her teammates embodied the fight for a new "rational dress" for women, where women campaigned for the right to wear clothes that allowed them freedom to move easily and take part in activities such as cycling or football.

This new style of dress, which Nettie was photographed wearing in some of the few images that exist of her in the 1890s, consisted of a cap, long-sleeved shirt, shorts, long socks and shin guards. It wasn't dissimilar to what the men were playing in during this time.

Nettie's team played their first official match in 1895 at Alexandra Palace in north London. Although they had been training with men's teams twice a week, they didn't have an opposition, so the team split into two and played North versus South. Over 10,000 people turned up to watch.

The newspaper reports said the match was terrible and that the crowd left at half-time. They complained that the standard was poor and the players didn't even know the rules. But Nettie didn't listen. The BLFC went on to tour the country playing matches against men's teams and attracting thousands of fans.

Unfortunately, in 1897, Nettie's team had to fold because they didn't have enough money to continue. However, the impact they had was huge. Other teams began to pop up around the country off the back of the success of the BLFC, and women's football continued to grow.

Nettie was determined to show that women's football was sport and entertainment, just like the men's game. She had fought for women's equality and she knew that football could be powerful in improving women's rights and position in society.

Her fighting spirit remains at the heart of the women's game. Players today still face similar challenges: to earn money for playing sport, to be paid equally with men's players and to be judged on their ability rather than their appearance. Thanks to the courage of people like Nettie, this generation of players is transforming the way the sport is viewed by fans.

LEGENDARY LADIES: DICK, KERR LADIES AND LILY PARR

Twenty years after Nettie Honeyball's British Ladies' Football Club was entertaining crowds up and down the country, another legend emerged in women's football. While Nettie was all about putting on a show, Lily Parr was an athlete. She was a superstar footballer who proved that women footballers were just as talented as men.

Lily was part of the Dick, Kerr Ladies team that rose to fame during the First World War. Dick, Kerr Ladies was formed in Preston, in the north-west of England in 1917. During the war, between 1914 and 1918, all men of a certain age were called up to fight against Germany. It was a big moment of change for society. To keep the country functioning, women started to do jobs that had always been done by men, such as farming and delivering post, instead of doing household chores and looking after their children.

Women began working in factories that produced weapons for the war. In order to keep their workers healthy and motivated, lots of factories founded sports teams. One of the most popular sports was football, and soon there were factory teams all over the country.

The Dick, Kerr & Co. factory was no different and women working there regularly played football in their lunch-breaks. After a bit of banter with the factory's men's team over a heavy defeat, Grace Sibbert, one of the keen women footballers, decided they should take on the men and play a game. The result of that match is unknown but it was the start of the Dick, Kerr Ladies team.

With the help of Alfred Frankland, who worked in the factory office, Dick, Kerr Ladies began to stage matches for charity. The first match was against another factory, Arundel Coulthard Foundry, and it took place at Preston North End's Deepdale stadium on Christmas Day in 1917. Over 10,000 people turned up to watch the match and Dick, Kerr Ladies won 4–0. The match raised money for a local hospital that was supporting wounded soldiers.

Dick, Kerr Ladies played in a distinctive kit, with black and white vertical stripes. At the time, they played wearing bonnets on their heads, in order to abide by the traditional modest dress of the time. Their boots were leather, as was the ball, which was very hard and heavy. It seems strange to think of women playing football in such clothing and shoes today.

Their matches may have been for charity but the performances were causing a stir. Dick, Kerr Ladies were defeating almost every team they were coming up against and a lot of that was down to Lily, who was their best player.

Lily grew up playing rugby and football with her older brothers. She joined Dick, Kerr Ladies at just fourteen and she played on the left-hand side throughout her time there, first as a left-back and then a left-winger. She was a tall and strong footballer and newspaper articles reported that she could tackle harder in games than most men. Her shot was so powerful that very few goalkeepers, male or female, could save it.

As no professional men's teams were playing during the war, women's matches were becoming great entertainment. Lily played in the record-breaking Dick, Kerr Ladies match that took place on Boxing Day in 1920. The match was between Dick, Kerr Ladies and local rivals St Helens Ladies, and it was staged at Everton's famous Goodison Park ground in Liverpool. Dick Kerr, Ladies' huge popularity led to a record crowd of 53,000 coming to watch.

At this point, the Dick, Kerr Ladies team were so popular, they were playing matches against international sides. A team arrived from France to play four matches in Preston, Stockport, Manchester and London and Dick, Kerr Ladies headed over for their own tour not long after.

The rise of women's football was happening at a time when women were slowly becoming more equal in society. Some women had been granted the vote in 1918. But the FA, the body in charge of football in England, was unhappy that so many people were enjoying the women's game. The powerful men who ran the FA seemed worried that the women's game was going to steal attention away from men's football which was restarting after the war.

> **FOOTBALL FACT**
>
> The FA (the English Football Association) was founded in 1863. It's the oldest football ruling body in the world. The FA is in charge of grassroots and professional football in England, writing and enforcing rules. The organization also looks after the national teams, including the Lionesses.

The FA decided to ban women from playing football in grounds affiliated with the FA, not long after the historic Boxing Day game that Lily played in. In 1921, the FA ruled that football was "unsuitable for females", claiming this was to protect women from the physicality of the game, but really it seemed like just another way to put women in their place in society. Without big stadiums for their fans, interest in the women's game trickled away. It would take until 2019 for that Boxing Day match attendance record to be broken in a domestic women's football game, when over 60,000 fans watched Atlético Madrid take on FC Barcelona at the Metropolitano Stadium in Madrid.

Women's teams carried on competing, but in the shadows without the crowds. Dick, Kerr Ladies changed their name to Preston Ladies in 1926 and still led the way. They tried to drive the creation of leagues and cups with other teams around England. They even flew over to the USA to play football against men's teams, on a trip that caught the attention of sports journalists and American sports fans.

Alongside football, Lily trained as a nurse. Lily wasn't just ahead of her time on the football pitch, she was also open about her sexuality at a time when it was illegal for men to be gay and there was prejudice around same-sex relationships, although the law didn't specifically reference women. Lily was open about her relationship with her partner Mary, and the pair worked at the same hospital.

Lily carried on playing despite the ban until she retired in 1950. She scored in her last match when she was 45. Her playing career lasted an astonishing 31 years.

FOOTBALL FIGURE

Lily retired with around 1,000 goals to her name, an unbelievable number that is impossible for most players — male or female — to achieve.

For many years, not many people knew of Lily's incredible achievements because there was very little public interest in women players. She became the first woman to be inducted into the National Football Museum Hall of Fame in 2002. In 2019, the museum unveiled a statue of her, the first of a woman footballer in the UK.

It would take 50 years for the FA to lift the ban on women's football and even longer for women's football to gain the respect of the men's game. The constant need for women players to prove society wrong hasn't disappeared. It still exists in some sections of the media, the public, the game and certainly on social media. Players today still have to battle stereotypes about women's football, but following Lily's courageous example from all those years ago, they are changing the game for the better.

CHANGING ENGLAND: GILL COULTARD AND THE DONCASTER BELLES

After the FA banned women's games from happening on its pitches, it became much harder for women to play organized football. And the celebrity and fame that had surrounded some teams during the First World War had evaporated. There was no glamour or glory for the women and teams who played during or just after the ban. Instead, it was all about playing for the love of the game. No one demonstrated this better than Gill Coultard, star of the Doncaster Belles, one of England's longest-serving captains and one of the country's most-capped players of all time.

> ## FOOTBALL FACT
>
> England wasn't the only country that had banned women's football during this time. Brazil, Belgium, Denmark, France and Germany all tried to stop women playing organized football. At the time, it was wrongly thought that playing sport was bad for women's bodies or would even impact a woman's ability to have children. There was sexism, which means prejudice and discrimination towards the opposite sex, around women in sport all over the world.

During the Second World War, between 1939 and 1945, men were once again called up to fight and women went to work in the factories. Despite the ban, teams were still popping up and games were played at unofficial venues. There were crowds, but nothing like during the First World War. In 1941, the National Service Act made unmarried women and childless widows aged between 20–30 liable for conscription (compulsory enrolment in the armed forces). Women therefore also played football for recreation while serving in the forces.

When the war ended, women were keen to keep playing and join teams. Matches were staged but it was still difficult to find pitches, get licences or referees.

Things were starting to change by the 1960s. Women were fighting for their rights and equality across lots of different parts of society. They wanted equal pay, better jobs and control over their bodies. Football wasn't going to be excluded from this fight. In 1969, the Women's Football Association (WFA) was launched with 44 member clubs all made up of volunteers. The WFA set up regional leagues and organized women's football spread around the country. But there was a growing frustration that teams couldn't get access to council pitches or good facilities because of the ban from the FA. Anger continued to grow among teams and players about how unfair it was. The pressure was growing on the FA to get a hold of the game to help it develop, and in some ways also control it.

Denis Follows, the then secretary of the FA, decided to intervene and end the ban. He believed in the right for everyone to play sport. In 1969, Denis wrote a letter to the WFA to let it know that the FA had decided to lift the ban. But it wasn't until 1971, 50 years after the 1921 ban, that the FA ban would be considered officially reversed.

The removal of the ban didn't immediately transform the game and women were by no means equal in the world of football. There was a long way to go on pay, as everyone was amateur – which meant they were playing for free – and media coverage was still minimal. But lifting the ban at least meant that players could get access to proper pitches and referees.

In 1971, the first Women's FA Cup final took place between Southampton Women's FC and Scottish team Stewarton Thistle at Crystal Palace Park stadium. Southampton beat Stewarton 4–1, with striker Pat Davies scoring a hat trick.

> **FOOTBALL FACT**
> The FA Cup is a historic cup competition to decide the best club in England, open to many different leagues. The first edition of the men's FA Cup took place in 1871 but the women's edition wasn't founded until 1970. The Women's FA Cup was run by the WFA from 1970 until 1993. The FA then took control of women's football in England, including running the cup competition.

The FA didn't take control of the women's game until 1993. There was a lot of distrust between the

WFA and the men in control of English football because of the ban. But as women's football was slowly given more of an official platform with proper leagues, teams started to emerge that would take the country by storm.

One of those teams was Doncaster Belles, who started life as the Belle Vue Belles in 1969. The team was set up by a group of women who sold raffle tickets at Doncaster Rovers men's games. The team started out by just playing small-sided games locally, but within a few years they started playing fixtures against teams outside of Doncaster. They decided they needed a new name that represented where they were from and decided on the Doncaster Belles.

It took a few years before the team started winning trophies, with their first regional league title coming in 1977. But once the Belles won their first Women's FA Cup in 1983, they couldn't stop winning. They were unstoppable because they had two of the best players in England at that time: centre-forward Karen Walker and midfielder Gill Coultard. They helped the Doncaster Belles become the queens of English football during the 1980s and 1990s.

Gill joined the Belles when she was just thirteen and played for them for the next 24 years. She started playing football with her brothers as soon as she could walk, and was part of a mixed team at primary school. But when Gill moved to secondary school, she wasn't allowed to play football with the boys and there weren't any girls' teams for her to join.

A teacher suggested Gill try out for the Belles, despite the fact some of the players were double her age. She soon became their key player. She was a superstar who was brave, tough and brilliant on the ball. She could score goals too. During her amazing career as an all-action midfielder, she won six Women's FA Cups and two league titles.

In total, she played over 300 times for her team. This was when women's football was amateur and no one was being paid to play. She had to squeeze in time to train and play alongside her full-time job at a factory. She played not for recognition or reward, but because football was her life.

Soon came the opportunity to represent her country. An official England women's team was formed in 1972 by the WFA. Progress was slow and steady as a handful of fixtures were played against other national teams. There wasn't the funding and support like there is today and everyone was an amateur or volunteer. Gill was first spotted by then head coach Martin Reagan when she was just fourteen. She began training with the England team, but Reagan was wary about throwing her into international football too early.

Four years later in 1981, at the age of eighteen, Gill got her first cap against the Republic of Ireland in a 3–1 win. Ten years later in 1991, Gill was made captain. Instead of having holidays, she used her time off work to travel the world playing for England. She loved leading her team into battle and always encouraged and supported her teammates, even if they were having a bad game. Hope Powell, who played alongside Gill and then managed England for thirteen years, called her a "world class player".

She was England captain for nine years to 2000.

One of her career highlights was making the final of the first European Championships for women's football in 1984. England lost to Sweden, but it was a huge moment for Gill and the team. She was even part of the first England team to play at a World Cup in 1995, the biggest international competition in women's football. She captained the team and scored two in England's opener, a 3–2 win against Canada.

Gill didn't win any major trophies with England, but she did get the honour of getting 100 caps, becoming the first amateur woman to reach that milestone. She retired at the age of 37, with 119 England caps to her name.

> ## FOOTBALL FACT
> A cap is given to a player when they make an appearance for a national team. It's not just called a cap, it actually physically looks like a hat too. Often players keep a collection of all their caps from historic matches or milestones they reach like 100 matches.

Gill played football before the glitz and glamour and media coverage, but her legend lives on. In

2021 she was made an MBE for services to football and she's known as one of the greatest players to ever play for Doncaster Belles. Gill and the Belles team will go down in history as one of the most successful sides the women's game has ever seen, alongside greats like Arsenal. They put women's football back on the map after a 50-year ban and a long time in the wilderness.

Gill was part of the international game before it went professional and one of the first Lionesses, although they weren't called that back then. (That name came later, after the Three Lions nickname for England was given a new identity for the women.) Gill was part of a "silent generation" of women players who didn't get much coverage or attention, but quietly paved the way for the success of players who came after her. Her legacy created the Lionesses that fans love today.

CHANGING THE WORLD: THE USA'S MIA HAMM AND THE '99ERS

Legends are born from famous moments in history. They are the true stories of individuals whose legacies have stood the test of time and have inspired generation after generation.

There is one particular team in football history that is legendary all over the world: the USA team from the 1999 World Cup. Nicknamed "the '99ers", this group of women not only won the world's biggest women's football competition, but they did it on home turf and in the process changed women's football in America and across the world, including for the England team.

The World Cup is the toughest competition

in international football. Organized by FIFA (Fédération Internationale de Football Association), football's global governing body, it's where national teams from all over the world meet to compete for one trophy.

The USA has been a leader in women's football since the 1990s. Historically football has been a sport that girls play from an early age in America, and it was common to see women's teams at university and grassroots level. In fact, women's football – or soccer as they call it – has always been more popular than the men's game.

A lot of the sport's success in the country is down to an important piece of legislation called Title IX, which was passed in 1972. It said that men and women legally had to receive the same amount of education funding and this included money for sports programmes at school and university. This meant universities had to develop high-level sport opportunities for women alongside opportunities for men, and a new generation of top athletes was born.

The USA's first major trophy came in 1991, when they won the first ever Women's World Cup in China. The team followed their World Cup glory with home success at the 1996 Olympic Games in Atlanta, where they took gold. But the 1999 World Cup was different; 1999 was special.

The team's members were described as the "most known unknown women" in America, because when they started the 1999 tournament, the elite international game hadn't yet taken off, despite the USA's previous success.

Even before the tournament kicked off, excitement started to build among American fans. As the tournament was being played at home, the young generation of girls who were playing football were excited to watch their home team play in stadiums all over the country. Fans started following the players around like they were celebrities and turned up to the training sessions holding signs with star striker Mia Hamm's name.

Mia was like nothing the world of women's sport had ever seen. She came from a big family and moved all around the world when she was young, as her dad was a pilot in the US Air Force. While living in Italy, Mia started playing football and soon her whole family were obsessed with the game. When she moved back to the USA she played for her school. Her talent kept growing, and by junior high school she was playing on a boys' team. Towards the end of her high school days, she was helping her school win national titles. She went to the prestigious University of North Carolina, winning four national championships in the four years she was there.

Mia made her international debut when she was only fifteen. She was a dynamite striker with an unbelievable goal-record. She was also a team player, but ultra-competitive and she loved winning. By the time the 1999 World Cup arrived, Mia was one of the biggest names in the sport. She had already broken scoring records, and had Olympic and World Cup titles to her name. Off the pitch, she was quiet and shy, and didn't necessarily want the spotlight, but her talent and goals led her to big sponsorship deals and fame.

The 1999 World Cup was one of the biggest women's-only sports events in the world at the time. The attendances prove just how huge it was. The opening match between the USA and Denmark was played in front of a capacity crowd of over 78,000.

The players had spent lots of time in the lead up to the tournament talking about selling out stadiums but they didn't actually think it would happen.

The stage was set and Mia was ready to deliver. She scored in the opening game against Denmark, which the USA won 3–0. In their 7–1 victory over Nigeria, Mia scored again, this time in front of 65,000 fans. The USA finished the group stage by beating North Korea 3–0 watched by 50,000 spectators. The feeling was starting to build that the USA could pull off something special.

The next challenge would be a quarter-final against Germany, one of the best teams in the world. It was a tough and tight match, but the USA managed to win 3–2 and continue their quest for World Cup glory.

This win set up a semi-final against Brazil. The match would be taking place on Independence Day, a public holiday in the USA, which meant everyone would be at home watching and 73,000 people would fill the stadium in California. The USA took an early lead in the game through Cynthia Parlow and then Mia helped take them over the line in the 80th minute when she was knocked down in the box and won a penalty that Michelle Akers converted.

The USA had made the final, but the hard work was only just beginning. They would be facing China, a strong team who had made the semi-finals of the last tournament. The excitement that had been building throughout the World Cup was reaching absolute fever pitch. By the time the final rolled around, the whole country had gone football mad.

The final took place at the Rose Bowl in California, one of the most famous stadiums in America, in front of 90,000, a record attendance at the time for a women's sports event.

> **FOOTBALL FIGURE**
> Only the unofficial 1971 World Cup final in Mexico City has had more fans with an estimated 110,000 people watching that game.

The team had the backing of all the fans in the stadium. The crowd was chanting "USA" and waving their flags and signs for Mia, desperate for the team to win. Mia had been all over the TV and newspaper coverage during the tournament and now all eyes were on her in the final.

The game was tense. The USA couldn't find a breakthrough, but neither could China even after full time, and an additional 30 minutes of extra time. The match would go to a penalty shoot-out.

> ### FOOTBALL FACT
> A penalty shoot-out is used to decide the winner of a match if the game is drawing after 90 minutes or extra time. It involves both teams taking five shots in the middle of the box from a spot that is twelve yards (eleven metres) away from the goal. It is one of the scariest things in football and even the best penalty takers in the world can get nervous and miss a career-defining penalty.

Things were neck and neck for the first two penalties: China scored then the USA equalized. Despite the pressure, the USA stayed calm. Then, in the third set of penalties, the USA goalkeeper Brianna Scurry guessed which way China's Liu Ying was going to shoot and saved her penalty.

Brianna pumped her fists in celebration – she knew she had given the USA a huge advantage.

They just needed to score the three penalties they had left. Next up was Kristine Lilly, she stuck away hers, giving the USA a 3–2 lead. Then, after a goal from China's Zhang Ouying, it was Mia. She could hear high-pitched screams as all the young girls in the stadium willed her to score. She stuck it away calmly into the bottom right corner and gave the USA a 4–3 lead. China converted their fifth penalty and that meant Brandi Chastain had the chance to bring it home for the USA and win the shoot-out 5–4.

Brandi had the expectation of the country on her shoulders, but she didn't look nervous at all. She did a quick run up and smashed the ball into the top corner. In front of 90,000 people, the USA had won the biggest women's football tournament in the world.

Realizing what she had done, she turned to her teammates and whipped her shirt off, swinging it around her head. Brandi then dropped to her knees. Her teammates came running over and she embraced them, throwing her arm in the air. Since that day, Brandi's celebration has been known as one of the most famous images in the history of sport.

Forty million Americans watched the final on TV. Everyone was behind the team and everyone wanted to be like the star Mia Hamm. The success not only changed the sport in America, but sent waves around the world. Suddenly other countries wanted to build their women's football teams and England were no different. But without Title IX and the university system of the USA which ensured equal funding for men's and women's teams, it would take decades for England to reach anywhere near the same level.

Mia and the '99ers showcased women's sport at its finest. They challenged stereotypes around women's football and what a female athlete looks like. They performed on the biggest stage, with no fear and inspired a generation of new players across the world.

FOOTBALL FIGURE

By the time Mia retired, she ranked third on FIFA's list of all-time goal scorers in international women's football with 158 goals in 276 appearances.

LEGENDARY LIONESSES

THE INVINCIBLES: ARSENAL'S WINNERS RACHEL YANKEY AND KELLY SMITH

While the USA were dominating international football, in England the club game was having its own revolution. In the shadows of the men's game, a new club dynasty, packed with exciting talent, was building. The success of this club would even challenge the legend of the '99ers.

In the early 2000s, women's club football was growing as more teams were created, but it was by no means mainstream. It was long before the Women's Super League launched and Women's FA Cup finals were held at Wembley. Men's clubs started launching women's teams or took on existing clubs and attached their name to them.

This meant the women's team shared the name, club badge, history and fan base. It didn't mean the women's team suddenly had access to the same budgets or even the club's stadium. Women weren't fully professional and they didn't receive the same access to coaching, good facilities or support.

One of the biggest clubs were Arsenal. Arsenal Women were launched in 1987 by Vic Akers, who was the men's team kit man. Vic was the manager of the women's team for 22 years and, in that time, he oversaw the winning of 36 trophies and completely changed English women's football. He took club football from something played in the park to packing out big stadiums.

Between 2003 and 2009, Vic's Arsenal went on an incredible run of 108 games unbeaten in league and domestic cup games. In this period, Arsenal won every single trophy in women's football.

Only a few teams in the history of football have ever been that unbeatable. Arsenal's men's team famously became known as The Invincibles after they went the entire 2003–2004 season without losing a match, but not many people know that the Arsenal women's team went a step further. They remained undefeated for six years.

In 2006–2007, Arsenal won all 22 of their league games, scoring 199 goals and conceding just ten. They became the first club to win a continental sextuple, meaning they won six national and international trophies in one season: the UEFA Women's Cup, FA Women's Premier League, Women's FA Cup, FA Women's League Cup, FA Women's Community Shield and London Women's Cup. Incredible!

But what made the 2007 season even more special, was that Arsenal became the first and only English women's team to win the top club trophy in European women's football: the UEFA Women's Cup, now known as the UEFA Women's Champions League. They hold the record to this day.

FOOTBALL FACT

The UEFA Women's Champions League, or UEFA Women's Cup as it used to be known, is the top women's football club competition in Europe. Organized by the Union of European Football Associations (UEFA), it started in 2001 and the format has changed over the years. Now, it involves a group stage involving sixteen teams, followed by two-legged knockout games, where the result is decided by the score across two matches, and a final.

There were two top England players who were key to Arsenal's success in 2007 and inspired a generation of players: Rachel Yankey and Kelly Smith.

Rachel was a tricky and stylish winger who was compared to some of England's greatest players, such as David Beckham. She had speed and pace, but huge amounts of skill too. She loved adding tricks and special moves to her game, like stepovers and cutbacks. She was ahead of so many others at the time because she was so technical. Women's football didn't have many showboat players, who do tricks during matches. The game was different then and lots of players hadn't had that technical coaching or training. But Rachel focused on those skills and wanted to use them to beat players.

> **FOOTBALL FIGURE**
> Rachel was one of the first women's players to become professional in England in 2000, which meant she was paid to play for her club Fulham.

Alongside Rachel in the Arsenal and England team was Kelly. She spent some time playing in America, but it was at Arsenal where she won the most trophies. Kelly was one of the greatest strikers in the history of the game.

Like Rachel, she played football at another level to the competition. She had a striking ability that others dreamt of. Free kicks, penalties, Kelly could do it all. She could hit the ball so hard that it was almost impossible for goalkeepers to save.

Together, Kelly and Rachel were a dangerous and dynamic duo and a terrifying prospect for any defenders.

The 2007 Arsenal team was one of a kind. It was full of national team captains from England, Ireland, Scotland and Wales, and some of the best women's footballers in the world. That group led the team on a magical journey in Europe that finished with an amazing two-legged (which meant the result was determined by the score across two matches) UEFA Women's Cup final win.

Rachel and Kelly provided the goals in the team, alongside Lianne Sanderson and Julie Fleeting. Behind them was a creative midfield that included Karen Carney and Gemma Davison, and important defensive foundations with goalkeeper Emma Byrne and rocks at the back,

Faye White, Anita Asante and Alex Scott. With all of that talent Arsenal made it through the group stages, quarter-final and semi-final to a final match against Swedish giants, Umeå. No one really expected Arsenal to win when they headed to Sweden – no English club had ever come close to winning the Cup. But Arsenal believed in themselves and knew they could challenge one of the best teams in Europe.

Kelly was suspended for the first leg, which made everyone a little bit nervous. They'd be without their star striker. But in the end, they didn't even need her, because all the way back from defence, right-back Alex Scott surged up the pitch and managed to score an incredible goal. The team would have a 1–0 lead heading into the second leg, which would be at Arsenal's home stadium Meadow Park.

Umeå came flying at Arsenal in the second leg, and they were defending for their lives. At one point a shot even hit the post and then hit Emma Byrne in the face. But Arsenal battled on and they clung on for a 1–0 win. They were European champions! The home crowd at Meadow Park couldn't believe it. They were the first English club to win the crown and Rachel and Kelly, along with some of their teammates, were the first English players to ever win it.

The achievement summed up an Arsenal team that was at the absolute peak of their powers, the best of the best across the board. It was going to be hard for Arsenal to continue at such a high level after reaching such dizzy heights in 2007. But they did, they went on to win more and more league titles and domestic cups. It wasn't until 2009 that their incredible unbeaten record, that stretched all the way back to 2003, came to an end. After 108 matches and a 51-game win streak, Arsenal lost 3–0 to Everton.

No team today is likely to be able to achieve what Arsenal achieved in those years. Now there's more investment in club football across Europe, with the competition at club level getting tougher and tougher each year. The game has developed around the world and therefore the talent pool has increased. Clubs are growing their own women's academies too in order to nurture home talent. But the Arsenal legend lives on, as does Kelly's and Rachel's.

Kelly played for Arsenal until 2017 when she retired after a 20-year career. She won five FA Cups with the club, the European title and six league titles. She was an England legend, holding the goal-scoring record and earning 117 caps. She played in two World Cups, four European Championships and even an Olympic Games.

> **FOOTBALL FIGURE**
> Kelly scored 125 goals for Arsenal and 46 goals for England, a record she held up until Ellen White broke it in 2022.

Rachel played with Arsenal until 2016. She left after winning nine FA Cup trophies and playing for the club over 190 times. She had 129 caps for England, and at one point was the country's most-capped player.

The success of Arsenal motivated other clubs to support their women's teams and set the tone for everything that we see today in the women's game.

Both Kelly and Rachel left a legacy that was far more than just trophies. They inspired girls across the country to play football. They were some of the first players to appear on TV screens and highlight reels and their talents turned them into global names in the women's game. Often you have to see in order to believe and Rachel and Kelly were idols for lots of players, including future England great Karen Carney who retired in 2019, and the current England captain Leah Williamson. The visibility of their brilliance changed women's football for ever as it gave young players something to aim for.

⚽ ⚽ ⚽

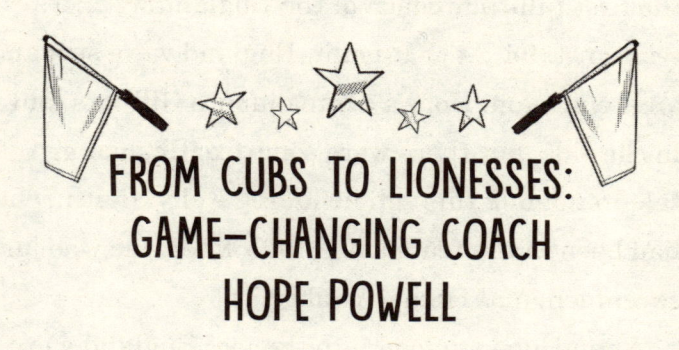

FROM CUBS TO LIONESSES: GAME-CHANGING COACH HOPE POWELL

The success of women's football isn't just down to incredible players such as Rachel Yankey and Kelly Smith. One woman changed English football through her pioneering coaching and leadership. Hope Powell was an inspirational player and coach who took the England team on a transformational journey from bare beginnings to tournament finalists.

Hope was an accomplished player, with 66 caps for England, and alongside Gill Coultard she was part of the first England team to play at a World Cup in 1995. But it was when she began coaching that she had a massive impact on the English game. It all started when she was appointed as the first full-time coach of the England women's team in 1998. At that point, England were still an amateur team. Hope's old teammate Gill was still in the side, but there were some exciting young talents coming through including Kelly Smith, who had been in the team since 1995 when she was just seventeen, and Rachel Yankey.

When Hope stepped into the job, England were not a good team. They were getting smashed 6–0 in friendlies against the USA and not performing well at major tournaments. To date, their best result was finishing as the runners up at the 1984 European Championship, when there were just four teams involved in the tournament. Since then, they'd only made it to the semi-finals of the 1987 Euros, had failed to qualify for other European Championships and not managed to go beyond the quarter-finals of the World Cup. Hope needed to get them competing with big footballing nations, such as the USA, Germany and Norway, but it wasn't just on the pitch where things needed to change.

> **FOOTBALL FACT**
>
> The first edition of the UEFA European Women's Football Championship, commonly referred to as UEFA Women's Euro, was organized in 1984 to find the best national team in Europe and just four teams took part. The competition has expanded since then, moving to eight teams in 1997, twelve in 2009, and sixteen in 2017, which it still is today. Germany have won the Euros the most times, winning eight titles, six of them in a row.

Hope soon realized there was a bigger challenge ahead of her than progressing through tournaments. If England were going to have any chance of winning on the biggest stage of all, Hope would have to fight for the men's and women's teams to be treated equally. The England men's team were all on professional contracts, received the best coaching and had all the physio and sports science support they needed. There were big broadcast and sponsorship deals in the men's game that brought in money, but women's football didn't have any of this.

Hope knew that if England were going to match nations such as the USA, who had the best set-up in the world, she would need to fight, just like the women who had come before her. She took on the FA, who were in charge of both the England men and women's teams, and asked for better facilities, a proper talent pathway and most importantly central contracts.

A central contract is a formal agreement between a player and the England team. It means they're contracted to the FA and are paid for doing the job of playing. For Hope's team this would mean finally being able to focus only on football. Up until then, a lot of players weren't being paid and therefore had to juggle other jobs in order to earn enough money. The time spent working was time away from training to become stronger and more technical athletes. If the team couldn't focus just on football, Hope had no chance of turning England into world-beaters.

It took years for Hope to persuade the FA, but she didn't give up. In 2009, her determination finally paid off. The first ever group of England players were given central contracts. Some, including Kelly Smith, were already playing professionally in America to a very high standard. But it changed everything for players such as striker Rachel Williams, who worked as a plasterer, and it meant she could get more rest and not work such long hours.

The central contracts came just in time for the 2009 Euros and Hope tried to get her team into the best possible shape. The championship took place in Finland and heading into it, Germany were the favourites to win the title. They had already won six of the last nine editions of the Euros, so unseating them from their throne was going to be extremely tough. England hadn't made it to a Euros final since 1984.

England didn't make the best start to the tournament, losing their opening game 2–1 to Italy. They followed that up with a narrow 3–2 victory over Russia and a 1–1 draw with Sweden. With twelve teams in the tournament, England just scraped out of the group and into the quarter-finals.

In the knockout rounds, it was more close calls. England defeated the hosts Finland 3–2 before narrowly beating the Netherlands 2–1 in extra time in the semi-finals. Kelly Smith put England in front in the 61st minute before the Netherlands equalized just a few minutes later. England couldn't find a winner in normal time but then, Jill Scott, with her height and power, headed in a corner late in extra time and sent Hope's England to the Euros final.

The team went wild, chasing Jill round the pitch as she ran off to celebrate. There was a reaction back home too because it was the first final the women's team had reached since 1984 and only the second time an England team had got to a final since the men's team won the World Cup in 1966.

Hope hadn't put too much pressure on her team to win the trophy. The main challenge was just getting out of the group, but now they had the final in their sights, they wanted to go and win it all. There was one thing in their way though, the queens of women's football at the time: Germany.

Germany hadn't just won Euros multiple times, they had won the World Cup twice. They were a dominant force in football. It was going to be a David versus Goliath match. But could Hope's team, just a few months into having the central backing from the FA, cause a huge upset?

It wasn't meant to be for England. Germany

took a 2–0 lead within the first 20 minutes of the final. Karen Carney and Kelly managed to get England back into it, but Germany quickly showed their dominance and experience, eventually winning 6–2. England put up a good fight and the final scoreline didn't reflect how well they had played against one of the best in the world.

After the final whistle, Hope and her players lined up to be awarded their runner-up medals with smiles on their faces. Even though the result was disappointing, they were still proud of what they had achieved. The march to the final had captivated the country. Hope's fight for central contracts for her players was vindicated. Her cubs had been transformed into Lionesses.

FOOTBALL FIGURE
Over 2.2 million people had watched England's tournament journey in 2009, a massive audience for women's football at the time, although nothing compared to the huge audiences for the 2022 Euros.

The 2009 Euros was the first chapter in a new era for England. There was an exciting feeling about what was ahead of them and what they might be able to achieve with Hope's backing and support. Hope coached the England team for fifteen years. In that time, she led England to two World Cups and four Euros appearances. She was also the head coach of Team Great Britain at the London 2012 Olympic Games.

She left the England job after the 2013 Euros when England didn't make it out of the group stage. England were the fourth-best team in Europe at the time but ended up with the worst record in the tournament. It was time for England to have a fresh start.

Hope finished the England job disappointed, but proud. The journey had ended on a sad note, but looking back over her time in charge, she could see how much she had changed the game.

When she first started, England weren't a world force. But Hope championed her team and told powerful organizations just how important it was that the England team and the domestic game received proper financial investment. Hope's work challenging authority, showcasing women's football and proving why it needed to be supported, was transformational. She set a path for England to thrive at major tournaments.

A few years after her departure, England made their first World Cup semi-final. Two more semi-final appearances followed and then in 2022 England won their first Euros. Hope's work and the progress England made shows that it doesn't just come down to what the players do on the pitch. Without her game-changing work off the pitch, there wouldn't be medals for the heroic 2022 Lionesses.

GOING FOR GOLD: TEAM GB AT THE LONDON 2012 OLYMPICS

The Olympic Games are one of the biggest events in sport. They happen every four years and involve thousands of athletes from over 200 countries. Not many countries get to host the Olympic Games, but the UK has been lucky enough to stage it three times.

The London 2012 Olympics brought millions of people together across the UK in a celebration of sport, culture and community. There was an exciting energy that swept the country and everyone was so excited about supporting British athletes.

An important aspect of an Olympic Games is also the legacy, which is all about what happens in the host country when the games are over. A legacy can be about participation, facilities and the local area, but it can also be about fans and visibility.

For women's football, London 2012 was a game-changer. Thanks to Hope Powell's continued efforts to get funding for the England team, it was the first time a Great Britain women's football team ever competed at an Olympic Games.

Women's football has been in the Olympic Games since 1996, when the USA won gold at their home games in Atlanta. The USA have dominated the tournament, also winning gold in 2004, 2008 and 2012. Norway and Germany are the only European nations to have won the gold medal. Canada won gold at the Tokyo 2020 Olympics (postponed until 2021 owing to the Covid-19 pandemic).

If the summer of 2022, and England's Euros success, will be looked back on as a moment that changed so much for English women's football, it was the 2012 Olympics and Team GB's women's team that really paved the way.

At the time of the games, the Women's Super League (WSL) had only recently launched. The league had eight teams and the majority of players were still part time, playing football alongside their regular jobs. Fans now watch the WSL week in week out, but at this point games weren't very well attended. The highest attendance was about 2,500 and one match in the first season had an attendance as low as 105 people. There wasn't much TV or media coverage either. But having a huge summer tournament on home soil could act as a massive boost for the WSL. It would put women's football on sports fans' radar.

FOOTBALL FACT

The Women's Super League is England's top women's football league. It started in 2011 and was originally a summer league, running between March and October, not in line with the traditional English football calendar. In 2017 it switched to align with other leagues and now runs from September until May. When the league first started it wasn't fully professional — there were semi-pro teams and lots of players were still balancing playing football with their jobs. There were eight teams in the first season but this has slowly increased to twelve. There is one champion crowned every season and one team are relegated to the second-tier and semi-professional championship. The league has been fully professional with players going full-time since 2018.

The Olympic Games are bigger than the WSL, the UEFA Women's Champions League and the Euros combined. Billions of people watch the games and the gold medal in women's football is seen as being as valuable as a World Cup title.

Team GB women wouldn't just be a football team, they would be part of something much bigger. A huge group of athletes was representing Great Britain across many sports including athletics, boxing, gymnastics and taekwondo. The players would stay in the athlete's village alongside sporting legends such as Sir Mo Farah and Dame Jessica Ennis-Hill. They would be part of the big opening ceremony and get to call themselves "Olympians". The prestige and the glamour would be like nothing England women's footballers had ever seen. Playing in the Olympics would be something none of the team had ever done before and probably wouldn't get to do again. They would be part of sporting history.

Hope Powell took on coaching duties for the Team GB squad. She filled it with exciting English talent including Alex Scott, Anita Asante, Fara Williams and Steph Houghton and Scottish players Kim Little and Ifeoma Dieke. All of the players felt honoured to be part of Team GB, but they had no idea what was on the horizon and how much the British public would want to support this team and follow women's football.

Team GB would be taking on Brazil, Cameroon and New Zealand in their group with matches at the famous Millennium Stadium in Cardiff and England's national stadium, Wembley, which had a capacity of nearly 90,000.

> ## FOOTBALL FACT
> Wembley is the home of English football. It's the home stadium for England's national teams and hosts the men's and women's FA Cup finals. It famously hosted the 1966 Men's World Cup final which England won, the men's team's only major tournament victory. In 2002, the stadium was knocked down and rebuilt on the same site. The new Wembley opened in 2007 and is famous for its arch that sits high above the stadium and can be lit in different colours.

The excitement around the Olympics was so great, everyone wanted to come and watch even if it wasn't a sport they normally supported. Most of Team GB's squad had never played in stadiums that big or in front of crowds that large.

Over 24,000 supporters came to watch Team GB's opening match against New Zealand. Steph Houghton secured a 1–0 win with a brilliant free kick that she curled over the wall and into the bottom corner.

The second match against Cameroon was a breeze, with England winning 3–0. This time as many as 31,000 had come to watch and Steph got on the scoresheet again, this time with a powerful strike from just outside the box.

The final group game was against Brazil, a strong football country who had a superstar player called Marta. She was very famous in Brazil and had been compared to one of the greatest footballers of all time, Pelé.

Brazil were the toughest opponents in Team GB's group. They'd won silver at the 2004 and 2008 games and could cause problems. The match was happening at Wembley, a stadium that had still yet to host the England women's team. Over 70,000 came to the match, by far the biggest crowd that any of Team GB had played in front of. Playing at Wembley was a dream for these players and something they never thought would be possible when they were growing up.

The noise in the stadium was like nothing the team had heard before. Fans had bought Team GB shirts and flags and they were all there to support women's football. The players didn't realize that there were so many fans who had been waiting to watch a women's team get the chance to play at Wembley. Team GB had the opportunity in a golden summer of sport to show just how exciting women's football was.

Team GB took the lead just two minutes into the game and it was Steph who scored her third goal in three games. Brazil failed to clear Kelly's corner and Steph managed to slip the ball around the goal and finish from a tight angle. She ran to the sidelines to be closer to the fans and slid to the ground in celebration. Her teammates jumped on top of her and she lay with her arms outstretched, absorbing all of the hugs and high fives. She had about eight Team GB players on top of her by the end. Steph closed her eyes in disbelief and let the noise of the crowd wash over her. Team GB had scored a goal at Wembley, the home of football. It was a dream come true. They held on to the match and went on to win 1–0.

Team GB were through to the quarter-finals and now had an army of fans behind them. Their next challenge was even bigger. They had to beat Canada in Coventry. The quarter-final didn't go to plan. Team GB were second best against an experienced Canada team and lost 2–0.

An even bigger crowd turned up to Wembley to watch the USA defeat Japan in the gold medal match. There were over 80,000 spectators at Wembley, not just a record for a women's football match in England, but the largest attendance ever for an Olympic women's football game.

The London 2012 Olympic women's football tournament and Team GB had proved that women's football was here to stay. Steph Houghton became a household name after her achievements during the tournament. A whole new fan base would also now want to go and watch England and the WSL.

The legacy for Team GB wasn't just about getting fans to games. It was also about inspiring girls to take part and dream of becoming

Olympians. The games succeeded at that too: Sandy MacIver and Jade Bailey were torchbearers during London 2012 and both of them have gone on to play in the WSL. MacIver has even played for England and went to Tokyo as part of the Team GB squad at the 2020 Olympic Games.

London 2012 was the beginning of a journey for women's football. Ten years later, England would finish off what those Olympians started at Wembley, with success at the 2022 Euros in front of another record crowd.

> **FOOTBALL FIGURE**
> Over 600,000 people watched women's football matches over the course of the London 2012 Olympics.

⚽ ⚽ ⚽

BRILLIANT BRONZE: FARA WILLIAMS AND THE FIFA WOMEN'S WORLD CUP 2015

Team GB's sensational summer in 2012 had been a special moment for women's football. But for the England team, things weren't going quite as well.

Since Hope Powell led the team to the 2009 Euros finals, England hadn't made it beyond a quarter-final at the World Cup or Euros. The start of the Women's Super League in 2011, the new women's football league, had brought a more organized and competitive set-up to the women's game in England. In a short time, the league had some fully professional teams, had been attracting sponsors and getting decent TV coverage. But the strength of the WSL hadn't yet rubbed off on the England women's national team.

> ### FOOTBALL FACT
> The Lionesses' nickname emerged in 2012 when the FA wanted to differentiate England men, known as the Three Lions, from the women's team during the men's European Championship in the summer of 2012. England Women had their own European qualifiers that summer and in order to give them their own identity the Lionesses' nickname was born. It started as a social media hashtag and then it developed into so much more: a brand, a community and a team.

The Lionesses' disappointing performance at the 2013 Euros in Sweden, where they didn't even manage to get out of their group, led to the departure of Hope Powell after fifteen years as head coach. It was a big change for England as all the squad had ever known was Hope and her leadership.

The new head coach was Mark Sampson. He had come from coaching women's club side Bristol Academy and led them to a runner-up finish in the WSL in 2013, which was the clubs best-ever finish. He also coached Bristol to FA Cup finals in 2012 and 2013. Sampson had two years to get England ready for the 2015 World Cup in Canada.

By 2015, the England squad was in exciting shape. Steph Houghton was captain. Alongside her in defence she had the experienced Laura Bassett, Alex Scott and Casey Stoney, as well as hotly tipped young talents Lucy Bronze and Alex Greenwood. The midfield was packed with players who had lots of caps for England including Jill Scott and Fara Williams. Up top, England had guaranteed goals with Ellen White, Lianne Sanderson, Eniola Aluko and a fresh-faced Fran Kirby, who was unknown in 2015.

For Fara Williams, this World Cup was particularly special as it was going to be her sixth major tournament with England. The centre midfielder was a key player with over 150 caps for England. She was one of the most experienced players in the team and was also the designated penalty taker, which was always important in major tournaments. She had been in the team for the 2009 Euros and with Team GB in 2012. At 31, Fara knew she wasn't going to have many more major tournaments ahead of her or many more chances to try and win something with England.

Fara had had a difficult life, but football had been an amazing escape for her. She grew up playing with boys and her raw talent got her a place in Chelsea's Under-14s at just twelve years old. She made her way up through the sides, but at seventeen she ended up homeless, after she fell out with her mum. Fara didn't see her mum for nine years and ended up sleeping rough, living in hostels, hiding it all from teammates and coaches. She made her England debut at the same time as she became homeless. Sometimes life was scary living alone and staying in unknown places. England coach Hope Powell was one of the few people she trusted and someone who really looked after her. Eventually a move to Everton, and the support of another coach Mo Marley, allowed Fara to finally settle.

Now Fara had a new England coach in Mark, but her goal was still the same. She really wanted to win something with England.

Given the last few years had been rocky, there wasn't pressure on England heading into the World Cup. The main aim was to see how far they could go. Things didn't get off to a good start in Canada. England lost their opening game against France 1–0. It seemed a big task for England to get out of the group stages. But they managed to get things back on track with 2–1 wins over Colombia and Mexico. Fara scored a penalty in the Colombia game and got her World Cup goal tally up and running.

> **FOOTBALL FACT**
> A penalty kick is a direct shot at goal that a player gets to take as a result of a foul or as part of a penalty shoot-out to determine the winner of a match. The kick is taken in the box on a spot that is marked twelve yards (eleven metres) away from the goal.

In the round of 16 they faced Norway, a highly rated and highly ranked team. England came from a goal down to pull off a 2–1 win and secure a place in the quarter-final against the hosts Canada. It would be very tough to take on the host nation in front of a sell-out home crowd that would be backing them all the way.

Getting to the semi-final would be a huge achievement. No England team, men's or women's, had made it to a semi-final of a major tournament since England men won the World Cup in 1966. All these years later, suddenly the England women had the opportunity to put English football back on the map.

England got off a brilliant start. Jodie Taylor put them in front and a few minutes later Lucy Bronze had doubled the lead. Canada got a lifeline just before the end of the first half but couldn't find a way back into the game and England made it through to the semi-final winning 2–1. England had done it!

Next they played Japan, who had won the 2011 World Cup. Only this match stood between England and the final. Even though the match was happening in Canada and the time difference meant that England fans would need to stay up past midnight to watch the game, lots of people were excited to tune in and see the Lionesses play. Fara and her teammates' journey had captured the nation.

England went a goal down in the first half, when Japan's Aya Miyama scored a penalty. But Fara levelled things up with her own cool, calm penalty just before half-time. England were still in the game and had a chance of winning when something completely out of the blue happened. In a freak accident, in the 92nd minute just before the game went to extra time, Laura Bassett slid to try and intercept a Japan pass into the box. But when she went to the ground, she clipped the ball into the air and it bounced off the crossbar and over the line to make the score 2–1. It was a heartbreaking and horrible way to lose the match. Laura was devastated and everyone rallied round her to make sure she was OK.

Even though England had lost there was still a chance they could come away with a medal and still be the first team to do so since 1966. England would be playing in a third-place play-off match against Germany, who had also lost their semi-final match.

A peak audience of 2.4 million had watched the semi-final in the early hours in England. There wasn't time to wallow, England had a job to do.

Things were tense from the very first moment of the game. Germany had a brilliant chance and England nearly went a goal down, but Steph just managed to clear a shot off the line. Neither team could find a breakthrough in normal time and the match went to extra time.

Finally, in the 108th minute, England got their chance. Lianne was brought down in the box and won England a penalty. Just like she'd done twice already in the tournament, Fara confidently stepped up to take it. She looked up at the goalkeeper to try and put her off and send her the wrong way. The referee signalled for Fara to go, she took a few quick steps and smashed it into the bottom corner.

She peeled off and pointed to the sidelines to celebrate with all of her teammates. England had to hold on to their lead for about ten minutes. Eventually the final whistle went and everyone ran on the pitch to celebrate. They had claimed the bronze medal.

It was an incredible moment for Fara. She had experienced plenty of heartbreak with England, but now she had scored the goal that won the bronze medal at a World Cup.

It felt like everything was changing. Team GB had woken up a nation with the Olympic Games and now England had followed that up with success in Canada. It wouldn't just be women's football fans paying attention, all of England would now be following the team's journey. The Lionesses had arrived on the big stage and the only way was up.

⚽ ⚽ ⚽

STANDING UP AND SPEAKING OUT: ENI ALUKO AND ENGLAND'S NEW DIRECTION

Standing up and speaking out is very important. Throughout history, people have come together to make a change by using their voices. Sometimes that can mean protesting: marching together with signs to draw attention to issues that they believe in. Or it can mean taking on big and scary powers on your own.

It's not easy challenging powerful organizations, but there are lots of people who have risked everything in order to do it. Eniola Aluko is one of those people. She spoke out against racism in the England team and changed the game as a result.

Eni was one of England's most successful footballers, playing as a striker for Chelsea and Charlton as well as the England team, but it was off the pitch where she had the greatest impact.

She was born in Nigeria and grew up in Birmingham with her mum, who was a nurse, and her younger brother Sone, who was also a very keen footballer and went on to play in the Premier League. Eni's dad was a politician in Nigeria and she spent time visiting him. She often found it hard to understand her identity and be accepted for who she was: a tomboy who was Nigerian and British with a passion and talent for football.

Eni loved playing football with the boys on her estate. It was where she felt most at home. Her talent was soon spotted by a club and she started playing for her local team Leafield Athletic Ladies. She then moved to a big local club Birmingham City, who had a thriving women's team. She ended up playing for lots of different clubs in England and the USA, but it was at Chelsea where she really made her name.

FOOTBALL FIGURE

Eni scored 68 goals in 158 appearances at Chelsea and won the Women's Super League and FA Cup twice.

Eni was part of the England team that made it to the 2009 Euros final and she represented Team GB at the London 2012 Olympic Games. She also won a bronze medal as part of the 2015 World Cup team. She earned 102 caps for England and scored 33 goals.

It wasn't just football that was a passion for Eni. Her favourite book growing up was *To Kill a Mockingbird*, a novel all about racism, prejudice and fighting for justice. She went to university and studied law and worked hard to balance her playing time with a career as a lawyer.

Eni was obsessed with the main character in *To Kill a Mockingbird*, Atticus Finch, a lawyer who has to represent a man who was falsely accused of a crime. From an early age, Eni saw the importance of challenging authority. Eni said that she "really liked the idea of having a voice for the voiceless, getting someone justice against the odds."

She tapped into her legal qualifications early in her England career when she helped negotiate a new central contract for England players, getting them better pay and better rights with the FA.

But that was only the beginning for Eni. Years later, she would become a whistle-blower, someone who reports wrongdoing at a place of work, after the England coach made racist comments to her and a teammate.

Eni reported what had happened to the FA and said that she felt like she was being bullied because she complained about the comments. At the time, the FA investigated but nothing was done. Even some of her teammates didn't believe her and sided with the manager. Eventually the FA made a payment to Eni, which Eni believed was to stop her from telling anyone about what had happened.

Eni was never selected to play for England again. She was one of the best players in the country at the time, was top-scorer in the league and was named in the league's team of the year. It seemed strange to her that she wasn't wanted in the England squad.

A few years after the incident, Eni decided to do something about her unfair treatment, even if it risked her career. She spoke to a journalist about what had happened and told them all about the comments, the investigation and the money.

Once Eni's story came out, the government decided to launch an investigation to find out what had happened and why the FA had not supported Eni.

Eni ended up being called to a government hearing and having to answer lots of questions under pressure. It was extremely scary but she was brave and determined to make sure the truth was heard, just like Atticus Finch, the main character of her favourite book.

Eventually, the FA apologized to Eni and her teammate over what happened. It may not have been complete justice, but Eni felt like she had stood up for what was right and put an end to a stressful period that had impacted her career. Eni's work led to the FA creating a proper policy for whistle-blowers so others could come forward in the future about bad things they had experienced.

Eni didn't stop there with her work for equality. She retired from playing, but started working in the boardroom. While at Aston Villa, she launched a special higher-education programme that allowed players to get extra qualifications so they were prepared for life after football.

Eni will be remembered for how she fought for justice and truth, taking on the all-powerful FA, but it's important to also remember how good she was as a player. She achieved great things and had moments of pure joy scoring lots of goals throughout her career and playing at the top of the sport. She scored a goal for England against the Netherlands where she dribbled past at least five players and then smashed it into the back of the net.

She was a brilliant footballer but she was more than just an athlete, she wanted to stand up for what she believed in, even if it meant not being able to play the sport she loves. Eni's fight for justice led to a better culture and environment for people working and playing English football. In 2020, the FA introduced a new diversity code which aims to address race and gender inequality in its leadership. However, since Eni and other players from her generation, such as Alex Scott and Anita Asante, hung up their boots the Lionesses have lacked diversity. All but three of the players in the 2022 Euros squad were white.

The FA is working to make sure that the England women are more diverse and everyone has the opportunity to play and can access the best academies and clubs. It's important that all girls get the chance to play and that the Lionesses represent women from different backgrounds.

⚽ ⚽ ⚽

GOLDEN TOUCH: LUCY BRONZE AND THE FIFA WOMEN'S WORLD CUP 2019

The Lionesses had made major progress by the time of the 2019 World Cup. Four years earlier at the 2015 World Cup in Canada, they had won their first major medal after finishing third. They also made it to the semi-finals of the 2017 Euros. Those impressive finishes had really lifted the team into the spotlight.

There was massive excitement about what England might be able to achieve at the 2019 World Cup. Could they go one step further and make it to the final or maybe even win the whole thing? The tournament took place in France in June and July. At the time, it was the biggest

Women's World Cup in the history of the game. Twenty-four teams took part, a record number, and for the first time Chile, Scotland, Jamaica and South Africa all qualified for the tournament.

Every team dreams of winning a World Cup, but this one felt different. There was more excitement around the tournament and therefore more pressure on the Lionesses. As the tournament was in France, lots of people would be able to travel to games and they would be easy to watch live at home on TV. It was the main sporting event that summer, it was the main football event of the year and everyone wanted to watch the tournament. It showed how much the game had developed since the 2015 World Cup when hundreds of journalists turned up to interview the Lionesses and head coach Phil Neville, who was a big name in the men's game, before the 2019 tournament even begun.

The tournament got off to a fantastic start for England. They got through the group stage with ease, with three wins out of three against Scotland, Argentina and Japan. Then they faced Cameroon in the round of 16 and won comfortably.

The next team they faced was Norway, who were highly ranked and rated. The team would need all their star talent to pull together if they were going to win the match.

One of the Lionesses' biggest and brightest stars was right-back Lucy Bronze. She had dreamt of winning a World Cup ever since she was the only girl playing in a boys' team when she was ten years old. Her love of football came from her older brother Jorge, and Lucy wanted to be just like him. Jorge never let Lucy win and it instilled a competitive spirit in her from an early age. She was strong and skilful and that shone through as her career went from strength to strength. Tough is actually Lucy's middle name!

Lucy was one of the most recognizable and experienced names in the England squad. She had won lots of trophies in the WSL with Liverpool and Manchester City, and also won the Women's Champions League with Lyon in France. She had been playing for England's senior team since she was 21. She had played in the 2015 World Cup, scoring two goals in the knockout rounds, and was part of the 2017 Euros squad.

Lucy was heading into the tournament with the world at her feet and a lot of responsibility within the England team. She was ambitious, but Lucy knew that winning the World Cup was going to take a whole team effort. She wasn't going to be able to do it solo, from her right-back position. She was a defender, so wasn't expected to score lots of goals, but Lucy was different. She always wanted to make an impact on the game.

Lucy was one of the best defenders in the world. She was extremely physical, tough, intimidating for attackers and immensely determined. Lucy had had several bad knee injuries over the years but none of those had held her back. She was exceptional at tackling and reading the game, working out what an attacker was going to do next.

As Lucy was a right-back, she also needed to be good going up the pitch. Lucy was quick, brave and brilliant at putting the ball in the box, but she could also finish too.

Lucy carried the team well going through the group stages. She used all her skills to give England the best foundation for the knockout stages. But Norway were a team that had been progressing just like England in recent years and would definitely be tough to beat. England needed to prove that they belonged in the semi-finals, and at the top of women's football, by beating a good team and beating them in style.

Lucy was feeling very confident and within the first few minutes of the match, she linked up with her teammate Nikita Parris to create a chance for England.

Lucy accelerated down the right, like there were rockets in her boots, and played a ball back to the top of the box where Ellen White and Jill Scott were waiting. Ellen took a swing at the ball and missed it, but right behind her was Jill. Jill slid the ball into the bottom corner and it bounced off the post and went in. England had the lead in the first three minutes of the match and Lucy had set up the goal.

Just before half-time, England took a 2–0 lead and Lucy helped set it up again. She connected with Nikita, and this time she played the pass that allowed Nikita to set up Ellen, who had a simple tap in. England were 2–0 up and absolutely flying. Lucy was playing so well, everyone she touched was turning to gold. Now she wanted a goal of her own.

In the second half she got her moment to shine. England had a free kick just outside the right-hand side of the box and Beth Mead was lining up to take it. Lucy signalled over to her to make sure she knew she was free, sitting at the edge of the box with no one around her. All the Norway players presumed Beth was going to send a cross into the box, but instead she laid it back and Lucy had all the time and space to take a shot.

Lucy hit the ball so sweetly it was like watching the perfect golf swing. The connection was pure power and precision. The ball flew into the roof of the net and Lucy, knowing she had scored an unforgettable goal on the biggest stage, stood with her arms outstretched waiting for her teammates to celebrate with her.

Lucy felt like she was the queen of football. She had entertained the world with her talents and England had announced themselves in the competition. They had made the semi-finals and the Lionesses were a team to be feared.

Lucy's goal would go on to be nominated as one

of the best in the tournament and she would take home the silver ball award for the second-best player at the World Cup.

Lucy stayed at Lyon for another year before returning to Manchester City in 2020. After two years, she made a big transfer to Barcelona, the Spanish champions, 2021 Women's Champions League winners and one of the best teams in the world.

Lucy's star has continued to shine and she's one of the biggest names in the women's game. At 31, she is still the starting right-back for England, and in the 2022 Euros she finally got to get her winner's medal as part of the victorious Lionesses side at Wembley.

FOOTBALL FIGURE

In 2019, Lucy was runner-up at the Ballon d'Or awards, given to the best players in the world, and in 2020 she won the FIFA Best award for being the best player in the world.

PENALTY PAIN: STEPH HOUGHTON AND THE FIFA WOMEN'S WORLD CUP 2019

Lucy Bronze's heroics guided England through to the semi-finals, but awaiting them in the next round was the most successful team in the history of the women's game, the USA.

England had never beaten the USA at a major tournament, but they felt confident this time. The Lionesses had a very talented squad, who had now been playing professionally for a number of years. The WSL had moved to a full-time league in 2018 which meant that players across the league, not just at top clubs, were training like full-time professionals. This had made the league more competitive and allowed players to get better and tougher match experiences. England's players had developed physically and technically and felt ready to compete with the super-experienced Americans.

The Lionesses had been in this position before, having made it to the semi-finals in 2015. That meant being in the final four of a World Cup wouldn't be such a scary or unknown prospect. But, having experienced so much heartbreak in 2015, they didn't want to go through that feeling again. This time, they wanted to be in the final.

The game would be significant for Steph Houghton, who had experienced plenty of ups and downs with England since becoming captain in 2014. Steph had achieved a lot with England and had been part of teams that had been to semi-finals, won friendly tournaments and even bronze medals, but she had never won a major trophy.

Steph was almost at the peak of her powers. She, like so many of the Lionesses' top players, had grown up in the north-east of England and started playing for Sunderland. It wasn't long before she made the move to the biggest club in women's football at the time, Arsenal. She won it all in London and then took the step to

Manchester City to become the club captain and launch the club's new, professional women's team.

Steph had played at the Olympic Games and had already got to 100 caps for England. She was one of the most experienced players in the squad and as the captain she was the team's leader.

Steph loved being captain of England. She felt so much pride every time she put the armband on and it was a privilege to be the one that got to lead the team out. She didn't take the responsibility of being captain lightly. She knew it came with pressure, but she loved setting an example to the rest of the team. Whether it was making sure her boots and kit were perfect or getting all the team to listen to the instructions of the manager, she knew how important it was to bring everyone together.

Steph was a central defender so she commanded the team from the back of the pitch. She would shout instructions, get players organized at corners and free kicks and also make sure everyone was focused.

She was brilliant at taking free kicks and penalties: it was one of her top talents. She also excelled at defending. She was tall, great at timing tackles and also sending accurate long balls up to her teammates. Steph had made a name for herself as one of the best defenders in the world but she wouldn't be able to beat the USA alone, she would need all of her team to be at their best.

Before the tournament even started, Steph said in an interview that she thought the Lionesses could "do something special" in France. Now the opportunity to beat the best team in the world was there.

The semi-final was taking place in Lyon in front of nearly 50,000. Because of all the USA's success in the tournament in the past, lots of American fans had travelled to support their team. They outnumbered the England fans in the stands and added an extra bit of pressure to the occasion.

FOOTBALL FIGURE

The USA have won four World Cups (1991, 1999, 2015, 2019) an unmatched record. They've also won gold at the Olympic Games four times and been champions of their region, the Confederation of North, Central America and Caribbean Association Football (CONCACAF), an incredible ten times. They're the most successful team in the history of the women's game.

Down on the pitch, the prospect of beating the USA was daunting. The USA had Olympic gold medallists and World Cup winners in their team. Competitiveness was in their DNA. Steph knew that her team would need to tap into something bigger, and find another level they may have never got to before.

The Lionesses didn't get off to a good start and within ten minutes they were a goal down. A ball came swinging in from the right side and Christen Press headed it straight into the roof of the net. The American fans roared and England felt deflated. But it was Steph's job to get them going again.

She shouted words of encouragement before the game restarted, asked them to believe in turning things around, and they did. Nine minutes later they had an equalizer, Ellen White, so clinical and reliable, tapped home Beth Mead's cross. England were up and running.

However, it didn't last long. Just over ten minutes before half-time, the USA were back in front again. This time it was their superstar striker Alex Morgan who headed the goal in. She found some space in between Millie Bright and

Demi Stokes and guided it into the net. Alex added the sucker punch to England when she mimed a tea-sipping celebration, poking fun at the English love of tea.

The USA were leading 2–1 but there was still lots of time for England to turn things around. Steph would need her team to stay focused and come out fighting in the second half.

They did. Jill Scott played a quick pass through to Ellen, who took one touch and smashed it home. Ellen turned to her teammates and did her customary goggles celebration, but things weren't even just yet. The referee went to check the goal on the video assistant referee (VAR) monitor and unfortunately Ellen's foot was inches offside. The goal wouldn't stand.

FOOTBALL FACT

The video assistant referee (VAR) is a system used in big tournaments and competitions to help referees make important decisions like penalties and offside calls. It's been used in FIFA events since the 2018 World Cup and now it's also used in the Premier League and Champions League. A form of VAR is thought to be coming to the Women's Super League at some point in the near future.

Steph and the team had to go again. Up the pitch they went once more and it was Ellen again with an opportunity in the 79th minute. The ball was played across the box by Demi and as Ellen waited for it, she was pushed in the back and went down. Steph screamed at the referee to give a penalty.

The referee blew her whistle and ran over to the VAR monitor to have a look. Steph knew that if the penalty was awarded, she would have to take it. Nikita Parris was the original designated penalty taker, but had missed two penalties earlier in the tournament. Before the match, head coach Phil Neville said that Steph would be called upon if they got a chance. After a few minutes, which felt like an absolute lifetime, the referee signalled for a penalty.

Steph's teammates trusted her and believed in her. She had a great penalty record and she had been practising all week in the lead up to the match. It was the biggest moment in Steph's career. This penalty could take the match to extra time and keep England's hopes of making a World Cup final alive.

Steph held the ball in her hands before she put

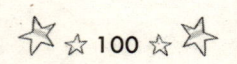

it down on the spot. She didn't want to rush it and she didn't want to change her usual routine. She placed it down and took a breath. With a short and sharp run up, she approached the ball and made contact. But, as soon as her foot hit the ball, she knew it wasn't a clean strike. There wasn't nearly enough power to send it past the goalkeeper Alyssa Naeher and she watched the tame strike go right into her hands.

Steph jumped in the air in frustration. That was the moment and it was gone. She didn't have time to stop and reflect, there was ten minutes to go and Steph still needed to try and lead her team.

England had nothing left. They couldn't muster any chances and their fate was sealed when Millie got sent off just before the end of the game.

When the final whistle eventually went, Steph dropped to her knees. The team had given everything, but in the moment that mattered, they just came up short. Her teammates came rushing over to pick her up and console her. She was heartbroken, but she was still proud.

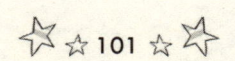

They had pushed the best team in the world all the way and that was special. Their World Cup journey may have ended but that was something they could take forward. Steph sensed something was changing for England and she hoped this was only the beginning. She would be proved right just three years later at the 2022 Euros.

Unfortunately for Steph, she didn't get a chance of redemption as an injury prevented her from making it into the England squad for the 2022 Euros. But the very best players know that you learn more from defeat than you do from winning. The 2019 loss inspired many of the victorious Lionesses in 2022. Players including Lucy Bronze, Jill Scott and Ellen White weren't going to experience that heartbreak again.

⚽ ⚽ ⚽

FOOTBALL FIGURES
The FIFA Women's World Cup 2019

- ⚽ Over one billion people watched the games on TV around the world.
- ⚽ The semi-final match between England and the USA was watched by a peak audience of 11.7 million people on BBC, a record at the time for women's football.
- ⚽ The final between the Netherlands and the USA was the most-watched women's football event of all time, with an average live audience of over 80 million.
- ⚽ Thailand were beaten by the USA 13–0 in a result that was the biggest loss in the history of the Women's World Cup.
- ⚽ Brazilian legend Marta scored her seventeenth goal across a consecutive five tournaments, which is the most that any player has scored at a men's or women's tournament.
- ⚽ The prize money for the 2019 World Cup was the most it had ever been at US$30 million (£25.9 million), but it was still much smaller than the men's World Cup, which had prize money of US$400 million in 2018.
- ⚽ American forwards, Alex Morgan and Megan Rapinoe, and England striker, Ellen White, were joint top-scorers for the tournament with six goals each, but Megan won the golden boot award as she had more assists.

TRIUMPHANT LIONESSES

THE UEFA WOMEN'S EURO 2022: TOURNAMENT OVERVIEW

The UEFA Women's Euro 2022 brought together sixteen of the best teams from Europe for one of the biggest competitions in the women's game. It was hosted in England in July 2022 and took centre stage during a summer that didn't have a major men's football event.

It was the second time England had hosted the Euros. The first time was back in 2005, when legends such as Kelly Smith and Rachel Yankey were playing, but it was very different then. In 2005, women's football in England wasn't getting coverage in newspapers or on prime-time TV. At the 2005 Euros, some matches had less than 1,000 fans at them.

Things were different in 2022. The Lionesses had become household names. They were all over billboards for the tournament sponsors, in major magazine features and on TV. Their faces were all over the huge Nike flagship store in London. The famous England white shirt had been given an update, a unique iridescent England crest that shimmered in the light. Captain Leah Williamson was photographed wearing it and the shirt flew off the shelves as everyone wanted to be kitted out like their heroes.

Tickets for the opening match sold out in a flash. Nearly 70,000 would be watching England's opening match against Austria at Old Trafford, one of the most famous stadiums in England. The quarter-finals, semi-final and final at Wembley also sold out. The Euros were the hottest ticket in town. Even for the warm-up games before the tournament started, the press boxes were full and the stands were bursting with fans wanting to catch a glimpse of the team.

The talk from the fans and the media was all about "football coming home". The Lionesses and their new coach, Sarina Wiegman, had to answer the same question at every press conference and media event. Could they do it? Every day they were reminded how much pressure and expectation was going to be on them.

Sarina reminded the media and her players to take everything one step at a time and not get carried away. Whenever she was asked about winning England's first trophy since the men's team won the World Cup in 1966, she would say they just needed to win six games: three group games, a quarter-final, semi-final and the final. The players were keeping calm too. It was tournament football and they knew anything could happen. Some of them had already learnt the hard way in World Cups and Euros with England in the past.

The excitement kept building right up to the opening game at Old Trafford, known as the "Theatre of Dreams" and home to Manchester United. There was so much expectation that this team was going to do what no other English women's team had ever managed and no England team in over 50 years. They would have all the support of the fans. Now it was up to the players to deliver on the pitch.

☆ THE SQUAD ☆

1. **Mary Earps** – Goalkeeper
2. **Lucy Bronze** – Defender
3. **Rachel Daly** – Defender
4. **Keira Walsh** – Midfielder
5. **Alex Greenwood** – Defender
6. **Millie Bright** – Defender
7. **Beth Mead** – Forward
8. **Leah Williamson** – Defender/Midfielder
9. **Ellen White** – Forward
10. **Georgia Stanway** – Midfielder
11. **Lauren Hemp** – Forward
12. **Jessica Carter** – Defender
13. **Hannah Hampton** – Goalkeeper
14. **Fran Kirby** – Forward
15. **Demi Stokes** – Defender
16. **Jill Scott** – Midfielder
17. **Nikita Parris** – Forward
18. **Chloe Kelly** – Forward
19. **Bethany England** – Forward
20. **Ella Toone** – Midfielder
21. **Ellie Roebuck** – Goalkeeper
22. **Lotte Wubben-Moy** – Defender
23. **Alessia Russo** – Forward

COACH WITH A PLAN: SARINA WIEGMAN

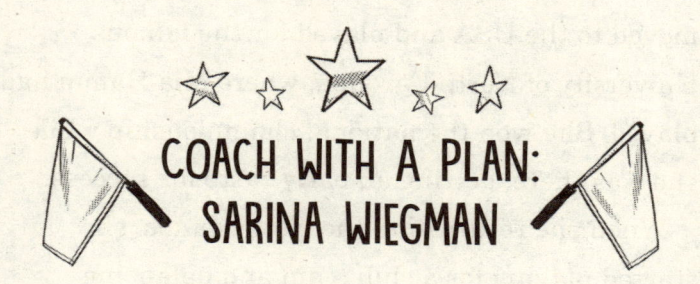

After England lost their third successive semi-final at the 2019 World Cup there was a growing feeling that change was needed. Initially Phil Neville stayed on as head coach, but he decided not to continue beyond 2021 and then moved to a new job in men's football. The search began for his replacement.

The next challenge facing the Lionesses was the 2022 Euros. England needed a head coach who had been there and done that. No one fitted that description more than Sarina Wiegman, a coach who like Hope Powell before her, transformed the Lionesses through her self-belief and ambition.

Sarina grew up in the Netherlands and loved football. She was so good at the game that she moved to the USA and played for the famous University of North Carolina, where Mia Hamm had played. She won the national championship while she was there, getting an early taste for success.

When she returned to the Netherlands, she started playing for a club team and balancing that alongside working as a PE teacher. Teaching provided the perfect foundation for her coaching. Sarina learnt how to plan, how to work with lots of different people and how to understand all the ways that players learn.

Sarina won trophies at club level and played for the national team too. She was also the captain, showing that she could lead a team. But it was when she turned to coaching that she really shone. Sarina was small, but feisty. She was direct and firm with her words, but never mean or rude.

FOOTBALL FIGURE
Sarina was the first women's player to earn over 100 caps for the Netherlands.

She started out coaching a local girls' team, but she quickly moved to coaching senior teams and eventually she made it to the big stage, coaching her country. She was initially just an assistant coach but she soon stepped up to the head coach role.

In 2017, when she became head coach of the Netherlands, there was just six months to go until the country was set to host the Euros. At the time, the Netherlands weren't one of the best teams in the tournament, but as they were hosts, they were still one of the favourites.

Going in, Sarina told her team they had nothing to lose, and they took her literally. The Netherlands won all of their games en route to a historic Euros victory. They were inspired by Sarina's vision and her tactics. She encouraged her players to support each other, not just play for themselves but to work together. She allowed them to believe in themselves and know that anything was possible.

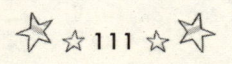

Managing the pressure and expectation that came with having a home nation in a tournament would come in handy a few years later when Sarina took over the England job. Not only were England hosting the 2022 Euros, Sarina had the task of trying to win the first major trophy since 1966. But she didn't know that yet. First, she had to navigate the 2019 World Cup with the Netherlands.

Could Sarina take them to World Cup glory too? The Netherlands had only ever qualified for one World Cup before, the 2015 tournament, where they got to the quarter-finals. Winning the trophy was going to be a big ask, but in a short space of time Sarina had transformed her team.

The 2019 World Cup got off to a great start for the Netherlands. Sarina's team continued their perfect tournament record, sweeping the group stages and making it to the knockout rounds with ease. They dispatched Japan in the round of 16 and then Italy in the quarter-finals. Sweden would be up next in the semi-finals and it would be the hardest game of the tournament so far.

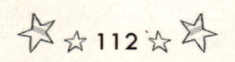

It was a tough and tight match. Both teams had to defend for their lives and the goalkeepers were the star players in the game. Nothing could separate the two teams and the match ended up going to extra time. Sarina made several substitutions to try and freshen up her team and bring some new energy. She brought on Shanice van de Sanden, a speedy and tricky winner and she instantly made an impact.

In the 99th minute, the Netherlands carved out a historic winning goal. Midfielder Jackie Groenen drove from the edge of the box and smashed a shot into the bottom corner. The goal sent the Netherlands through to the final for the first time in their history. It was incredible achievement. Sarina wasn't emotional after the final whistle though, she was calm and collected because she knew this was where they belonged.

Now Sarina had made back-to-back major tournament finals, but could she win back-to-back trophies too?

The Netherlands faced the USA in the final, the most successful team in the history of the sport and a country Sarina knew well from her playing days. Sarina was aware of how athletic and skilled the players would be, but she believed in her team. The final would be a historic moment for Sarina and her opposition manager Jill Ellis as it would be only the second time that two women had coached in a World Cup final.

Sarina knew it would be a huge challenge and, in the end, the game was one step too far for her team. They lost 2–0 and the amazing journey was over. It was a gutting defeat, but Sarina had taken her team from outsiders to the best in Europe and one of the best in the world. She had made a name for herself as one of the most impressive coaches in the women's game.

She had caught the attention of England too. Sarina got the head coach job and took over Lioness coaching duties in September 2021, just under a year before the 2022 Women's Euros in England. She had a mammoth task to take England from three-time semi-finalists to winners, but if anyone could manage the pressure of coaching a host nation in a home tournament it would be Sarina.

From the first moment she started, the media were asking Sarina about winning the 2022 Euros and "football coming home". Sarina was clear that they would focus on doing everything they could to win, but it would be about taking one step at a time.

> **FOOTBALL FACT**
> When talking about the England national team, the media often talk about "football coming home". This is a reference to a famous song called "Three Lions" released in 1996 about the long wait for England to win a trophy in football.

She got off to a brilliant start winning all of England's 2023 World Cup qualifying games at the end of 2021. The next challenge was the Arnold Clark Cup, a friendly tournament where England would play some of the best teams in the world: Germany, Canada, the current Olympic champions, and Spain.

England won the competition with an unbeaten record, beating Germany 3–1 in the final match, a perfect warm up for the Euros. A hard-fought 0–0 draw with Spain in England's second match also showed just how England could match some of the best teams in the world. Spain are known for their amazing passing and technical ability and the fact England managed to keep them at bay was a huge confidence boost.

Thanks to Sarina, England were heading to

the Euros as one of the favourites. Sarina knew that meant lots of pressure and expectation, but she had been there and done that with the Netherlands. If anyone was up to the challenge of winning England's first trophy since 1966 and bringing football home, it was Sarina. And she had a squad of talented Lionesses, just as keen to make that dream a reality.

⚽ ⚽ ⚽

GOLDEN GIRL: BETH MEAD

Bouncing back from setbacks is very important for professional footballers. They will face barriers, but they will have to learn how to overcome them. It might be that they get a bad injury or fall out of the manager's starting line-up. But it's important that they don't give up and they keep working hard.

No one embodies that better than striker Beth Mead, who went from not making the England squad in 2021 to being England's best player at the 2022 Euros.

Beth grew up playing football with boys and like many of the current crop of Lionesses, she didn't really have a choice. It didn't matter because she loved being rough and tough. Parents would laugh at her when she arrived at the pitch, but Beth's teammates knew how good she was. As soon as the game started the laughing would stop because Beth was the best player on the pitch.

> **FOOTBALL FACT**
>
> Lots of the Lionesses began their careers playing football with boys. This was because girls' teams didn't really exist, so if girls wanted to play competitively and develop their skills they needed to play with boys. The new generation will have different opportunities to play because the number of teams around England has exploded since the Lionesses put women's football on the map.

Sometimes it was scary playing with boys who were much bigger than her, but whenever Beth was worried, her dad would tell her: "The bigger they are, the harder they fall." She learnt not to let her fears hold her back. If she got knocked down, she would bounce straight back up.

Resilience is essential in football. Resilience is about coming back from setbacks and building mental strength. Beth had tapped into her resilience plenty of times throughout her career. She moved to play at bigger clubs in bigger towns, hours away from her family. But every step of the way, at Middlesborough, Sunderland and Arsenal, whenever she faced an obstacle, her mum and dad pushed her and her confidence and self-belief grew.

Beth knew that to be the best she would need to push herself and step out of her comfort zone. Attackers like Beth have to take risks. Being a forward means you need to be brave, take on defenders and go for scoring opportunities when they come. Sometimes you will make mistakes and miss the target, but everything is an opportunity to learn and get better.

At Sunderland, Beth was the star striker, scoring 77 goals in 78 games. After she moved to Arsenal, she had to adjust because she wasn't the main striker any more. When Vivianne Miedema – the Dutch superstar – arrived, Beth had to become a winger, playing on the right-hand side of the pitch. She took on the challenge and overcame it, cementing a place for herself in the team.

Beth made her England debut in 2018 and

soon she was scoring goals for her country. In 2019, while on tour in the USA with England, she scored a stunning goal in a match against Brazil and followed it up with a goal against Japan too. She was becoming an important player for England and although she didn't start many games at the 2019 World Cup, she was still a key member of the squad.

But, in 2021, after Phil Neville left, England had a new manager, Hege Riise, who had been a big player in Norway and would be temporarily in charge until new coach Sarina Wiegman arrived. Hege dropped Beth from the team. She was told her performances weren't good enough. The decision meant she would miss out on going to the Tokyo 2020 Olympic Games with Team GB.

Beth was very upset, but she knew this was going to be another barrier she was going to have to overcome. She knew if she could showcase her skills on the pitch for Arsenal, she would be picked for England again.

Beth took on the challenge and had an amazing season. She won Arsenal's player of the season award, scored fourteen goals and had nineteen assists. Her performances got her straight back into Sarina Wiegman's England team and she was ready to take her form into the 2022 Euros.

The Lionesses' opening match was against Austria at Old Trafford, Manchester United's famous stadium. The game was sold out – there would be almost 70,000 people in the stadium – the biggest crowd Beth had ever played in front of. She was scared and nervous, just like when she was younger. However, Beth knew her family would be watching in the stands and they would give her the confidence she needed to perform well in the match.

Just before the game kicked off, there was a massive fireworks display. The noise from the fans was deafening. Beth couldn't see any of her teammates through the smoke cloud from the fireworks, but she could see the lights of people's mobiles phones taking pictures of the historic moment. Everyone was excited and, most importantly, they wanted to see England win.

Beth knew she just needed one chance to get England off to the winning start that everyone wanted. England were the home team and Beth was the in-form player. She was under pressure, but she was so confident she felt like she could take on anyone.

It didn't take long before a chance came her way. In the sixteenth minute, Fran Kirby ran towards a bouncing ball and in the corner of her eye she spotted Beth making a run in behind the Austrian defenders. Beth had timed it perfectly so she wouldn't be offside.

Fran gently lifted the ball over the Austrian defenders and Beth watched it sail over their heads and onto her chest. She controlled it, trying to get just enough power so that it would bounce in front of her and not into the hands of Austrian goalkeeper, Manuela Zinsberger.

The bounce was perfect. Beth had about half a metre to now finish the job and score England's first goal of the tournament. She pulled her trusty right foot back and chipped the goalkeeper.

The ball hung in the air and all the noise suddenly disappeared, there was silence. Beth was sure it was going to make it over the line. It hit the bar, Beth winced, but then as it came back down it moved over the goal line. Beth was sure it was a goal and her teammates were celebrating too. The referee paused, checking the VAR which would tell her if the goal had gone in. She finally signalled for the goal. Beth had done it.

She punched her arms in the air and clenched her fists. Her teammates surrounded her in the box, jumping on her in celebration.

Beth's goal was the only one of the match and the 1–0 would give England a crucial win to start the tournament confidently. There was a long road ahead, but this was step one for Beth and the Lionesses.

⚽ ⚽ ⚽

THE GIRL WHO BEAT THE BOYS: ELLEN WHITE

Record-breakers exist in every sport. They're the ones who smash the targets set by the sportspeople who came before them. Ellen White was born to be a record-breaker.

The England striker grew up in Kent and was obsessed with football. She started playing with her dad, brother and sister in the back garden. She played netball and did athletics too, but football was her main love. She even tried to play football with her pets!

It wasn't long before Ellen joined a local boys' team. Ellen loved playing with the boys and they loved having Ellen on the team. She was a brilliant striker. She'd fly through defenders and slice through the ball like butter, perfectly placing it into the back of the net. She was brave and had no fear.

When she was nine, Ellen's league said she couldn't play any more. Even though she had scored 100 goals for her team and was the best player, she wasn't allowed to carry on playing with boys. Ellen was upset, but she had just been scouted for Arsenal's academy so knew her football dream could stay alive.

While at Arsenal, Ellen learnt her best skills. She was relentless on the pitch. Defenders didn't know what to do: she would move around and be impossible to mark and was able to finish from anywhere. She also became famous for her work ethic. She is one of the hardest working players in women's football. She's a team player and always works hard, making sure she gives everything for her teammates.

Ellen played for lots of different clubs including Arsenal, Chelsea and Manchester City, but it's with England where she really made her mark.

Her England career got off to the perfect start in 2010, when she scored against Austria in her first ever game and after that she never looked back. Ellen won England Player of the Year in 2011, was part of the England team that finished third in the 2015 World Cup and made it to the semi-finals of the 2017 Euros and 2019 World Cup.

She couldn't stop scoring for the Lionesses and she was quickly heading towards beating the England record of 46 goals set by legend Kelly Smith. In 2021, 11 years after making her first appearance for England, Ellen scored her 48th goal for England in a friendly match against Latvia. She had made history, but there was one thing she still hadn't done: win a home tournament.

> **FOOTBALL FIGURE**
>
> Ellen's hat trick against Latvia made her England's highest goal scorer, with 48 goals in 101 appearances. The match ended 20–0 which broke England's previous record score in a competitive win, a 13–0 victory against Hungary back in 2005.

Ellen headed into the 2022 Euros having scored only four goals for Manchester City all season, her lowest for a club in a very long time. But she knew that when she played for England it was different. It was the most amazing feeling in the world playing for her country and putting that white shirt on, with the three lions on her chest. She also had the trust of her manager Sarina Wiegman. It's very important for a player and coach to trust each other, especially in a tournament, where every game and every moment matters so much.

The first game against Austria at Old Trafford passed in a blur. Ellen started the match but she didn't have that many chances to score. England won the game, but Ellen was a bit disappointed. She knew that with her impressive record there would be an expectation from fans and journalists that she should be scoring in every game.

England's next match would be against Norway, the hardest opponent in their Euros group. England had beaten them at the 2019 World Cup, but they were a strong team and no one was taking anything for granted. The match would be played in Brighton in front of 30,000. Ellen was ready to prove a point to the doubters who thought at 33, she didn't have what it took any more.

The game kicked off and Ellen could sense fear in the Norwegian players. They seemed nervous, but she wasn't. Within ten minutes, Ellen had won England a penalty. It was a textbook move from her, adjusting her body to get round a defender and forcing them to make a mistake. Georgia Stanway stepped up and stuck the penalty away. England were off to the perfect start.

Just a few minutes later, they would get a second when Lauren Hemp flicked the ball into the back of the net. England were flying and Ellen wanted to get on the scoresheet. If this was going to be a big win, she had to score.

All of Ellen's experience told her that Norway were a wounded team and she needed to pounce. She spotted an opportunity as one of the Norwegian players played a loose pass back to her teammate. Ellen pressured the player and used her strength to push her off, winning the ball about 30 yards (27 metres) from Norway's goal. She looked up and only had one thing in her mind: score. She dribbled the ball forward, with nothing in front of her but the goalkeeper. She edged closer and closer to the goal and once she got in the box she released her classic right-footed shot in the bottom corner.

Ellen had finally got her goal in the tournament and she had silenced the doubters. She pulled out her famous celebration, putting her fingers round her eyes like goggles and the crowd roared.

Not long after, England had another goal and then another! It was 5–0 within 38 minutes. The fans were going wild in the stands, but Ellen was focused. There were a few minutes to go until half-time and still time for her to get another goal.

Fran Kirby made a blistering run down the right-hand side and had clear space in front of her. Ellen made a dash for the box and screamed to Fran to cross it in. Fran played the perfect ball right into Ellen's path and Ellen stretched out a leg to guide it into the back of the net. She had her second goal.

The half-time whistle went and England were 6–0 up. It was better than any of them could have dreamt.

The game would finish 8–0. It was a stunning victory for England over their group rivals and one of the top 20 teams in the world. The result took the fans and the media by surprise, and it certainly woke up any of England's opponents who may not have been sure just how good this team were. The Lionesses and Sarina Wiegman were now full of confidence and ready to take on anyone.

Ellen felt like she was dreaming. She had waited so long to play in a home tournament, with her friends and family all in the stands. She'd played for England for twelve years and never won anything, but maybe this time the Lionesses would finally have what it took to win.

⚽ ⚽ ⚽

EXTRA-TIME EXCELLENCE: GEORGIA STANWAY

England's stunning victory over Norway took all of the country and the footballing world by surprise. No one expected England to beat one of the top twenty teams in the world by such a huge scoreline. The Lionesses were already one of the favourites to win the trophy, but after that massive win, the expectation from their fans got even bigger. Suddenly they seemed unstoppable.

England finished the group stages with a comfortable 5–0 win over Northern Ireland in Southampton. They finished as top of their group and technically went through to the quarter-finals with an advantage. But awaiting England in the next round were Spain, who had finished runners-up in a very tricky group with Germany and Denmark.

Spain had headed into the tournament as one of the favourites, but just before the Euros kicked off, their star player, Alexia Putellas was injured. Alexia was the best player in the world and had won all the big awards, including the Ballon d'Or, which is given to the best men's and women's player every year. Without Alexia, Spain weren't the same team, but they were still dangerous.

> **FOOTBALL FACT**
> The Ballon d'Or is an annual football award given to the player who has performed the best over the previous season. It literally means "Golden Ball" and was first awarded in 1956 to England player Stanley Matthews. The women's version of the prize was first awarded in 2018. From the England team, both Beth Mead and Lucy Bronze have been runners up for the prize and previous winners include Alexia Putellas and Megan Rapinoe.

England were feeling confident heading into the quarter-finals. Why wouldn't they be? They had won all their group games, scoring fourteen goals without conceding any. Some of the goals and performances had been incredible. The home fans were buzzing, there was a positive feeling in the whole country and nothing was going to get in their way.

One of the best performers so far had been Georgia Stanway. Georgia grew up in Cumbria, in the north of England. She started playing for Blackburn Rovers before she was spotted by Manchester City, a big club in the Women's Super League. She made her City debut when she was just sixteen and within a month of playing in the first team, she was already scoring goals. She was so confident and that came out on the pitch too.

Georgia was a brave, commanding and composed central midfielder. She made her England debut when she was nineteen. In a short space of time, she had already gained lots of experience and played for England at the 2019 World Cup and for Team GB at the Tokyo 2020 Olympic Games.

Georgia had learnt some important lessons in her short career already, such as how to control her energy and make sure her frustrations didn't turn into fouls. There had been moments when she hadn't been able to balance her energy and enthusiasm. When she was younger, she would let her annoyance in games get the better of her and she got sent off a few times. But now she had matured and, at 23, she was becoming one of England's best players.

During the Euros, Georgia had been playing as a defensive midfielder. This meant there was even more pressure on her to not make any mistakes, as she was the last player that was protecting the defensive line. If she slipped up, she could leave her teammates exposed. But Georgia had been pretty much perfect so far, even scoring a penalty in England's 8–0 thrashing of Norway.

Her skills and patience would be tested massively when England faced Spain. Spain were famous for holding on to the ball and tiring opposition teams out with endless possession. England would need to get used to not having the ball and waiting for an opportunity rather than trying to force it. There wouldn't be the space for them like there had been in the other games. Spain's players were amazing on the ball and very good at pressuring their opponents into making a mistake. Trying to win the ball back off them was like trying to catch a fly – they were so good at escaping.

The quarter-final was taking place in Brighton, where England had smashed Norway. The fans had been really loud during that match and Georgia and her teammates were hoping for more of the same. The noise of the home crowd had made such a difference during the tournament, it lifted the team and gave them so much confidence.

The fans delivered from the first whistle, chanting, "It's coming home!" Every time England got on the ball the noise would lift. But England didn't get much of the ball. Spain were in their element.

The first half ended 0–0 and it was the first time in the tournament that England hadn't scored in the first half. Spain were trying their best to cause an upset and there would be work for the Lionesses to do in the second half.

Leah Williamson, the captain, and Sarina Wiegman, the head coach, had to keep everyone on track and focused at half-time. England were still in the game and had everything to play for.

Ten minutes into the second half, the worst-case

scenario happened: England went a goal down. Spain found some space on the right-hand side and they managed to take the ball past Georgia's teammate Rachel Daly, causing panic in the rest of the defence and then Esther Gonzáles slotted the ball home.

The home fans were stunned. The game wasn't meant to happen like this. England were meant to be flying through this tournament with ease, not having to come back from a goal down. The volume in the stadium became even louder.

Georgia and her teammates tried to stay positive. There was still over 30 minutes to go in the game and they didn't need to panic. There was enough time to turn things around. But, just after the game restarted, Spain had another chance, again from the right hand-side. Mary Earps, the England goalkeeper, just managed to stop a shot from going in. But Georgia began to worry.

England needed to get control. As time ticked on, it felt harder and harder to find a way back into the game. Georgia could sense the crowd panicking as England ran out of time. If they lost this match, their tournament was over, they would be knocked out. England tried to stay composed and keep working hard. Finally, things began to calm and England found a rhythm, but there still wasn't an opportunity to score an equalizing goal.

Just a few minutes from the full-time whistle, the chance finally came. Georgia sent the ball out wide to Beth Mead, who whipped the ball into the box. Alessia Russo headed it down and Ella Toone finished it. The crowd went wild. Georgia had never heard a noise like it. England had the equalizer in the 84th minute. Now the game was theirs to win. The fans were going wild.

At full time, the score was 1–1. The game would go to extra time to find a winner.

Georgia was sure she could be the one to win the game for England, and in the 96th minute her chance came. England were revitalized. They could sense Spain were being overwhelmed by the momentum that England had and the noisy crowd behind them.

England suddenly had more energy than they'd had all game. They were chasing the ball around and forcing mistakes from Spain's players. One of those mistakes allowed Georgia's teammate Keira Walsh to play the ball to Georgia about 45 yards (41 metres) from the goal. Georgia took a touch to bring the ball out of her feet and looked up towards the goal.

As Georgia drove forwards, all the Spanish players ran away from her, almost deserting her. She had so much space, there was no reason to pass it, she could go on and score herself. She continued to dribble on and as she got within about 25 yards (23 metres) of the goal, she decided to launch her shot. She put all the energy she had left into right foot and then made contact with the ball, trying to get as much power behind the shot as possible. As the laces of her boot kicked the ball, the connection felt perfect. The ball swerved and curved in the air, making it even harder for Spain's players to track. Georgia watched it sail past the Spanish goalkeeper and into the top left-hand corner. She had scored! Another deafening roar came from the crowd. England just needed to see out the rest of extra time and they had all of the crowd willing them along. It made them feel unstoppable.

When the final whistle blew a huge roar went up. Sarina, so normally cool and calm on the sideline, let out a huge cheer and waved her arms in the air. Georgia jumped on her teammates to celebrate and waved to her family in the crowd as the stadium DJ blasted classic England songs like "Three Lions" and "Sweet Caroline". The team did a lap of honour, drinking in the atmosphere.

It felt like a turning point for the Lionesses. It was just a quarter-final win, but it felt like so much more. There was still a semi-final and final to go before England could get their hands on the trophy but they had come from a goal down and pulled off a huge win against one of the best teams in the tournament and it was all thanks to Georgia's brilliant finish. It was a life-changing moment for her and the team.

⚽ ⚽ ⚽

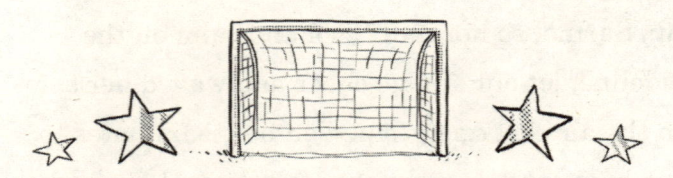

THE BACKHEEL THAT STUNNED THE WORLD: ALESSIA RUSSO

Women's football has come a long way since the 50-year ban that stopped the game's development in England. The game had to fight for decades to get investment in coaching, facilities and player contracts. Women's football still doesn't receive anywhere near the same level of investment as the men's game, but now that more players are able to go professional, their technical ability and skills have been transformed.

Nothing proved this more than a goal that stopped the world in its tracks during the 2022 Euros. That goal came in the semi-finals against Sweden from Alessia Russo.

Alessia grew up with her two brothers, Luca and Giorgio, in Kent. Football had always been in her family. Alessia's grandfather moved to England from Italy and became obsessed with Manchester United. Her dad, Mario, played semi-professional football and was the record goal scorer for the Metropolitan Police team.

When she was growing up, Alessia had no option but to play football. Her dad made it non-negotiable. In the garden with her brothers, Alessia would have to play every position: goalkeeper, defender, striker. She started playing properly when she was five, in the local team her dad coached. Like many of her teammates, she then moved on to play with boys. Alessia and her dad would get a few funny looks when they turned up to games, but it wasn't long before Alessia settled in her striker role and became the team's top-scorer.

She moved to play for Charlton and then Chelsea before she decided to head to the USA and play for the University of North Carolina, one of the best universities for women's football in the world. Alessia was a very talented striker at UNC, scoring 28 goals in 57 appearances. She was good at getting round defenders, very good at finishing and had brilliant acceleration.

Alessia had played for England at all junior levels. Just before she graduated from university, Alessia decided to head back to England and play in the WSL for Manchester United. She wanted to play professionally and also try and get into the England senior team.

By 2021, she had one cap to her name, but had only played a few minutes. She wanted more: she wanted to get into the England squad for the 2022 Euros.

Alessia's unique ability was her bravery. She liked to be aggressive and direct. She would pick up the ball and head straight towards the goal. She could smell out an opportunity. Most players didn't believe in themselves like Alessia did. She always trusted herself to beat an opposition defender and have the skill to score a goal.

Alessia was feeling confident heading into the 2022 Euros and she made the squad after good performances for England and Manchester United. She would be behind Ellen White in the team selection. Ellen was England's record goal scorer and the favourite in the number 9 role, which is the central striker position.

Alessia didn't get many minutes as England began their Euros quest with a win against Austria. But as the tournament went on, Alessia was getting more and more time on the field. She still wasn't unseating Ellen as the starting striker, but she was showing how important she was for the team.

In England's tense battle against Spain in the quarter-final, Alessia held off several Spanish defenders to allow her teammate Ella Toone to find a last-minute equalizer that kept England in the tournament. Without Alessia's strength, the Lionesses could have been knocked out.

England were nervous heading into the semi-final against Sweden. They had only just made it through their quarter-final and the nation's enthusiasm and confidence following that huge win over Norway had dampened a little bit. England realized that they weren't just going to walk their way to a European title, they were going to have to fight for it and beat some of the best teams in Europe.

Sweden were one of those teams. They had reached the final of the Tokyo 2020 Olympic Games the year before, beaten England in the third-place play-off at the 2019 World Cup and been near the top of women's football for the last few years.

England hadn't been to a final since 2009, when they lost in the final of the Euros. Some of the more experienced players in the squad had now made it to three semi-finals in a row but had never won one.

The semi-final was taking place at Bramall Lane stadium in Sheffield, a venue Sweden had already played in twice during the Euros. Although England fans dominated the stands, Sweden had good support with them too and they were making plenty of noise. Alessia was starting on the bench.

There was a nervous atmosphere in the stadium before kick-off as everyone knew what was at stake. It was a historic moment for England and a huge opportunity. An initial roar at kick-off quickly evaporated as Sweden made a good start and almost scored when a header from a corner nearly hit the bar. The crowd made a huge "ooo" sound and England fans instantly became twitchy. Was the dream going to end here? The Swedish attacks kept coming and Alessia looked on nervously from the bench.

After absorbing the pressure, England slowly got a grip of the game. Towards the end of the first half, Lucy Bronze found some space on the right-hand side, and whipped in a cross that Beth Mead brought down with her right foot. Beth turned and smashed the ball into the back of the net. The pressure lifted and England had taken the lead.

The half-time break followed not long after Beth scored. More of the same was needed in the second half and it arrived quickly. In the 48th minute, Lucy headed in a corner and England took a two-goal lead. They had even more breathing room.

In the 57th minute, with England 2–0 up, Alessia replaced Ellen as a substitute and went up front. England were flying now and had all of the possession. They continued to push for more and were deep in the Swedish half of the pitch.

FOOTBALL FACT

A substitute is a player who doesn't start a match but comes off the bench for a team to replace another player. A team can make a different number of substitutes depending on the competition or tournament. Sometimes it's a maximum of three, five or occasionally, in friendlies, it's even more.

Keira Walsh grabbed the ball, and looked up to see where her teammates were. She played a pass to Fran Kirby on the left-hand side who then played the ball across to Alessia. She struck the ball towards goal but it was saved by the feet of Swedish goalkeeper Hedvig Lindahl. The ball bounced back out to the right-hand side of the box and Alessia ran towards it.

She was sandwiched between two Swedish defenders with her back towards goal. It was an impossible angle from which to try and get an effective shot. But what if she hit it with the back of her foot? What if she backheeled it? It's one of the most impressive skills any footballer can pull off and to do it on the biggest stage would be quite something.

Alessia didn't waste any more time, she pulled her right leg out and pushed it back towards the ball and the goal, trying to get as much power on the ball as possible. She made good contact and it went past one Swedish defender and through the legs of Lindahl.

There was a moment of shock as everyone realized what Alessia had just done. The noise from the crowd was like nothing she had ever heard before, piercing and high-pitched. Alessia put her two arms high in the air and ran towards the corner flag. Her teammates followed her in amazement at what had just happened.

Alessia had just scored one of the most incredible goals ever, not just in the history of the Euros, but in women's football. She had made sure England's place in the final was secured. With her teammates by her side, she celebrated on the pitch, dancing, singing and hugging her family in the crowd. England were well and truly on their way to the final. And not just any final: a first major final since 2009, a home final and just one game away from winning the tournament.

⚽ ⚽ ⚽

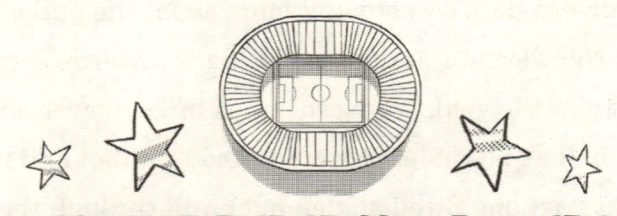

THE MOMENT THAT STOPPED THE NATION: CHLOE KELLY

Footballers spend years practising for big moments, but there's nothing that could have prepared striker Chloe Kelly for the moment that would change her life and the history of England women's football. After losing three major tournament semi-finals, England were now about to face Germany in the finals. They were going to be playing at Wembley, in front of nearly 90,000 people, most of whom would be supporting England.

On the day of the final, it was all anyone could talk about. The Lionesses were all over the radio, TV and newspapers. Thousands of people turned up to Wembley early to soak up the atmosphere and the whole area was packed with England fans.

It wasn't going to be an easy game for Chloe and her Lioness teammates. Germany were one of the best teams in the tournament and they had had plenty of success in past Euros. No England team — men's or women's — had won the Euros. In fact, the Lionesses were aiming to be the first England team to win a trophy since England's men's team won the World Cup in 1966 at Wembley. The whole team and their coach, Sarina Wiegman, had been dreaming of this moment, but for Chloe the day had an extra-special significance.

> **FOOTBALL FIGURE**
> Germany have eight Euros wins, two World Cup titles and an Olympic gold medal.

Chloe grew up in the shadows of Wembley in Ealing, west London. Living just a few miles from the famous stadium, Chloe dreamt of one day being able to follow some of her footballing heroes and play under the arch. She used to get the bus from Ealing to the stadium on the day of a big cup final. She'd buy a programme, soak up the atmosphere, then jump back on the bus and head home, hoping that one day she would be on that programme.

Chloe was from a football-loving family with five brothers and a sister. It was loud and busy at home, but football brought everyone together and they all supported Queens Park Rangers. Even though Chloe was the youngest, she could hold her own in the family football matches. Any spare moment she had, she spent playing football with her brothers.

Chloe's brothers never made it easy for her. They used to play in the local football cages and she would get pushed around, tackled and wrestled for the ball. In those moments she learnt all her best lessons: the freedom of doing skills like stepovers and other tricks, scoring goals and never getting a moment to rest.

FOOTBALL FACT

Cage football is a fast-paced game often played in a cage with walls on a small-sided artificial pitch. It's a high-intensity version of football and it encourages skill and technique development.

At school, she played with the boys too and it wasn't long before Chloe got to live out her dream and play for QPR. She had all the skills that are needed in an attacker: she was quick, agile and played as if the ball was stuck to her feet. Her talents were quickly spotted by Arsenal and she soon moved to their academy.

Chloe made her Arsenal debut when she was seventeen and scored just 22 minutes into the game. She was already showing signs of being a star. From Arsenal, she moved to Everton and then Manchester City. She made her England debut at 20 and was knocking on the door for more appearances in the national team.

It had been an exciting and successful couple of years for Chloe, but at the end of the 2020–2021 season, something terrible happened. When stretching for a ball in a game for Manchester City, Chloe injured her leg badly. She had to have an operation and she wasn't able to play for a very long time. She was going to miss competing for Team GB at the Tokyo 2020 Olympic Games and it looked uncertain if she would make the England team for the 2022 Euros.

She was heartbroken. Chloe knew she needed to give herself the best chance of coming back and making the team. She spent months not playing and having to slowly work her way back to fitness. She did boxing to keep fit and then eventually got back on the grass. Less than a year after her injury, Chloe would step back on the pitch for Manchester City and eventually she made her comeback for England too and was selected for the 2022 Euros squad.

Chloe knew that she probably wasn't going to start many games throughout the tournament, because her teammates Beth Mead and Lauren Hemp were in such good form, but she wanted to be ready when she was called upon. Like Jill Scott, she started the final on the bench. It was huge for her to be back at Wembley, where all her football dreams began.

The German squad was strong. Their star players, defensive midfielder Lena Oberdorf and attacking midfielder Lina Magull, could cause all sorts of problems. But there was a lucky break for England as Germany's best attacking player, Alexandra Popp, was injured just before the game kicked off and she wasn't able to play. She had been Germany's best player all tournament and she had scored six goals just like Beth Mead. But even without Alexandra, Germany were still a fantastic team.

The first half went by and it was tense. Both England and Germany were trying to find a breakthrough and take the lead but the defences were so strong, there were very few chances. It was 0–0 at half-time but head coach Sarina Wiegman didn't panic. She knew she had strong players to sub on, such as Chloe and Jill Scott and strikers Ella Toone and Alessia Russo.

Sarina didn't make any changes until the 55th minute, when Ella came on and replaced Fran Kirby. Seven minutes later, Ella got a golden chance to put England in the lead. Keira Walsh picked up the ball from just outside England's box. She looked up and could see Ella charging forwards. Keira played the perfect pass into her and Ella just had to chip it over the German goalkeeper. Ella took a small touch and then released the shot. The ball seemed to linger in mid-air as Chloe and all her teammates watched it fall into the back of the net in slow motion. England had the lead in the Euros final and there was just over half an hour to go.

Germany weren't going to go down easily though, they were going to fight as much as they could to still win this final. They kept knocking on the door and testing England's defence and goalkeeper, Mary Earps.

Chloe came on in the 63rd minute and her substitution was greeted by a huge cheer from the crowd. Everyone knew what she had been through to get to this moment. Chloe knew that this was a chance to be part of history, just like she had dreamt when she was a little girl.

As Germany were pushing and England were clinging on, Chloe's main job was to help England hold on to the lead and win the game. But the pressure was growing and eventually England couldn't hold on any more. In the 79th minute, Lina Magull scored a brilliant equalizer, flicking in a shot at the near post. Germany were right back in it and the match was going to extra time.

Before extra time started, Chloe huddled with her teammates and they all looked into each other's eyes. No one was nervous, there was confidence beaming from all of them. Chloe knew that if the opportunity came, this team would score and win the trophy.

The first half of extra time flew by and still no one had found a goal. The team just needed one more push. They had fifteen minutes to find the winning goal and stop the game going to penalties. As the clock ticked on, Chloe could feel her heart beating in her chest.

In the 110th minute they won a corner. Chloe knew this was a massive opportunity. Lauren Hemp would take the corner and Chloe knew that with Lauren's delivery, she just needed to be ready for when the ball dropped.

The ball was sent in by Lauren and headed towards goal by Lucy Bronze. Lucy's header fell at the feet of Chloe. She twisted and turned to wrestle off the German defender and get her body facing the goal. She waved a foot at it, not really making good contact, and her shot was blocked by the goalkeeper. Chloe thought the moment was gone, but the ball bobbled back towards her, she would get another try. With one last stretch,

Chloe pushed a leg out and managed to poke the ball. In slow motion, she saw the ball roll into the back of the net.

Chloe grabbed her shirt, looking at her teammates in disbelief. She paused, she wasn't sure if the referee was going to call a foul or disallow the goal. She turned and looked at the referee, waiting, was it OK? Did it count?

After a few seconds, the referee signalled for the goal and Chloe could finally celebrate. She whipped her shirt off and waved it around over her head, a look of shock and amazement on her face.

Chloe ran around the pitch with her shirt in the air, her teammates chasing her like a game of tag. She made it to the sideline where she was mobbed by the substitutes and coaches. She'd done it, she had scored a goal, at Wembley in a major final.

Once the dust settled, England had a job to do. They would need to hold on and defend for five minutes.

Eventually the final whistle blew. Chloe took a moment to let it sink in. She puffed out her cheeks and caught her breath as some of her teammates dropped to their knees. After a few minutes, she let herself realize what she had achieved. England were European champions and the girl from Ealing had scored at Wembley.

⚽ ⚽ ⚽

SUPER SUB'S LAST HURRAH: JILL SCOTT

Football is England's favourite sport. Everybody follows it, millions play it and hundreds of thousands go and watch their teams play every weekend. It was a huge deal for the Lionesses to have made the final. The last time an England women's team had been in a final of a major tournament was the 2009 Euros, twelve years earlier.

That final took place in Helsinki in Finland, in front of just under 16,000 fans, nothing like the crowd that would go to Wembley. It was England's first taste of a final, but it was a difficult game for the team. They were outplayed by an impressive Germany side, eventually losing 6–2 to one of the biggest and best teams in European football. So when England faced Germany again in the 2022 Euros final, it felt like history was repeating itself. For one player, Jill Scott, this feeling was even stronger. She was the only player remaining in the squad who had played in the 2009 Euros final and was desperate for England to win.

Jill was one of the most famous and popular players the England team have ever known. She grew up in Sunderland and was a massive Sunderland fan. She used to get the bus to the Stadium of Light to watch their games. She loved collecting all the programmes.

One day, when she was five, she went up to a group of boys and asked to play football with them and she never looked back. Soon, Jill was appearing in the local paper and everyone was hearing about her talents. She kept playing and was winning player of the match trophies at all her tournaments.

But like so many of her teammates, Jill was told that she had to stop playing with boys. She was so upset, she cried on the sofa all night. Her mum was determined to find her a new team and make sure that she didn't give up on her dream. She went on to play for Sunderland, and by the time she was nineteen she had made her England debut.

She quickly became a fan favourite for her personality and her attitude. Jill was tall and glided through the midfield with ease, but she was also a tough tackler and hard worker. She was the total package. Whenever she came on the pitch, she would give everything. But she also played with a smile on her face. Jill loved to joke around with teammates and opposition players and make them laugh, and she loved pulling pranks on people too.

Jill got to see it all playing for England. She travelled the world, playing in four World Cups, three European Championships and two Olympic Games. She had seen the team go from those early underpaid days to become a professional and slick operation.

> **FOOTBALL FIGURE**
> Jill played for England for over eighteen years and won 161 caps for England.

But even though Jill played for England for such a long time, she never managed to win a major trophy. The best she had was her bronze medal from the 2015 World Cup. By the time the 2022 Euros came along, Jill was 35. She knew that this Euros was going to be her last chance to win something. Jill had decided she would retire after the tournament, but she hadn't told anyone yet.

She hadn't played much of the season heading into the Euros because she'd been injured. Right up until the last moment she was pushing to be fit enough to make the squad. She was so nervous waiting to find out, but she made the team, and it meant she would be heading to her fourth European Championship and tenth major tournament with England.

Jill played less than 30 minutes in the lead up to England's final. She was coming on as a sub and just adding some experience in England's midfield but she wasn't playing a starring role in their journey on the pitch. But it wasn't just about Jill's contributions on the pitch, she was a leader off it and someone other players looked to for advice and guidance.

Jill was more excited than anyone when England made the final. She had waited her whole career for this. Finally, she was going to get the chance to put things right in a final, in front of nearly 90,000 at Wembley. She never thought she would see that many people at a women's game when she was growing up, let alone get to play in it.

England's coach Sarina Wiegman picked the same team for the final that had started every match. Jill was on the bench, but she was OK with that as she knew she wasn't the best player to do the job that the coach needed. Jill would still play a part, encouraging her team from the bench, and she knew if she was called upon, she would be ready.

Jill took in every moment of the final like she was a fan. From arriving at Wembley on the bus, to stepping out on the grass to do the warm up and then singing the national anthem. She wanted to make sure she remembered every second.

Jill exploded off the bench when Ella Toone gave England the lead in the 62nd minute. She thought it was the winning goal, the goal that would finally give her a gold medal. But Germany got themselves back in the game through Lina

Magull and Jill felt sick with nerves.

She kept warming up with the substitutes, in case she was going to be called upon. In the 77th minute, Sarina signalled to Jill to get ready to come on. She would need to play in extra time and make sure that England won this game.

As Jill replaced Georgia Stanway, there was a huge cheer. The crowd knew how important this game was for Jill, they knew how long she had waited for a moment like this, and they loved her.

Jill ran on and instantly got stuck in, causing some problems and getting into a bit of a tussle with some German players. Jill had her game face on and she was going to play like she always did, tough and determined. As extra time went on, Jill tried to encourage her teammates and guide them with her experience.

Finally, the opportunity came and England had a corner. Jill was in the box as the ball came in and she watched as Chloe Kelly ran towards the ball. Everything flashed by in her head, the days playing in Sunderland as a kid, all the years driving around playing football after a day of full-time work. When she looked up, she saw that

Chloe had got the ball into the back of the net.

She ran towards Chloe to celebrate but both of them quickly turned around to the referee to check that the goal had been given. A few seconds went by where no one quite knew what was going on but finally she blew her whistle and Jill could celebrate. Chloe was waving her shirt in the air and Jill and all the players followed behind her.

The score was 2–1 with five minutes to play. Jill knew now that England were going to win. She believed in the defence and goalkeeper Mary Earps and knew they wouldn't concede. Jill needed to use all her experience to help England get over the line. She battled with her teammates to keep the ball in Germany's half and stop them getting up the pitch and getting another goal.

Finally, the final whistle went and the gold medal was hers. Jill ran up to her teammate Keira Walsh, who had been one of the team's best players in the tournament, and thanked her for all her amazing performances. Then, as the rest of the team were celebrating, Jill quickly ran to the changing room. She wanted to send a text to an old coach, Mo Marley, who coached Jill at Everton and England and someone she wanted to thank for taking a chance on her. She texted her "We did it Mo", and then ran back out to be with her teammates.

England captain Leah Williamson lifted the trophy high in the air and quickly handed it over to Jill and her teammate Ellen White, who was also retiring. They were one of the first people to get their hands on it and the cold medal felt amazing in Jill's hands. She didn't want to let go.

The gold medal round her neck that she had waited so long for felt so heavy, but incredible. Jill didn't want to leave the pitch, she sat on the grass and breathed it all in.

Jill wanted one last run on the pitch, to finish everything where it started, on the grass, just running. She turned to her teammate Lotte Wubben-Moy and one of the England coaches and asked if they would do some sprints with her. They said yes and Jill led them on her last run, with a gold medal around her neck.

⚽ ⚽ ⚽

THE CAPTAIN WHO BROUGHT FOOTBALL HOME: LEAH WILLIAMSON

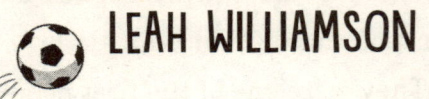

One of the most important roles on a football team is the captain. Captains need to make sure everyone is working together and they need to be at their best when others might be struggling. Captains aren't necessarily the most talented players on the pitch, but they are always good leaders.

Not every player dreams of being a captain, but every player dreams of lifting a trophy. That feeling of grabbing the cup in front of an adoring crowd that's singing your name. The feeling of joy as you raise it high into the air as confetti shoots into the night sky and fireworks explode in the distance.

Footballers also dream about experiencing that special moment at Wembley, England's national stadium. But for women's football that dream was never a reality, because when they were growing up, girls and women weren't lifting trophies at Wembley, they weren't on TV, on the front of newspapers or playing in front of thousands. England captain Leah Williamson changed that at the 2022 Euros.

Leah grew up in Buckinghamshire, and started playing football by chance. One day, at the end of a gymnastics session, her coach threw a ball down and she started playing with it. All the girls in her gym class ran around chasing the ball, but Leah was different, she wanted the ball at her feet. When she got home from gymnastics, she asked her mum if she could play football. The problem was, Leah's parents couldn't find a team because all the boys' teams in her local area said they didn't let girls play.

Leah's parents kept searching and eventually a friend of her mum's said that Leah could join a boys' team if she was good enough. It didn't take long before Leah was the team's star striker. While the boys on Leah's team were warm and welcoming, the parents from opposition teams used to say horrible things about her. "I don't think they wanted their boy to be embarrassed by a girl," Leah said.

Leah didn't let any of these nasty experiences stop her from chasing her dream, she was brave and determined. All of the tough times playing with boys helped her become a stronger person and Leah managed to block out the negative comments.

Leah learnt some of her best skills playing with boys. She had to be strong, physical and show great courage. The boys didn't give her any time to adjust so she needed to think under pressure, an important skill for all captains.

Not long after starring in her local boys' team, Leah moved to Arsenal, where she's been ever since 2006. She didn't stay a striker, moving into midfield and then eventually central defence.

At the age of just seventeen, Leah made her Arsenal debut in the biggest club competition in Europe, the UEFA Women's Champions League. She replaced Arsenal legend Rachel Yankey and it wouldn't be long before she became a legend herself.

Just as she was climbing up the ranks at Arsenal, Leah began to get noticed by England too. She played for every England junior team, from England Under-15s all the way to Under-23s.

Years later, Leah was given the captain's armband for the 2022 Euros by head coach Sarina Wiegman. Leah would have the expectations of the entire nation on her shoulders. When she got the captaincy, Leah said that it was "the biggest honour in football". Her picture was all over the newspapers and TV screens and there was a huge amount of pressure for her as the face of her team.

Leah was so proud, but she knew it would be a big duty to captain England in a major tournament. Only a few England players in football history had ever done that and one of the most famous was Bobby Moore, who captained England in the 1966 World Cup final at Wembley, and won. That was the ultimate goal for Leah.

A good captain needs to set an example. They need to block out the noise and make sure their team stay focused. From the start of the 2022 Euros, Leah made sure that the team weren't distracted by the excitement of the fans and everyone singing "Football's Coming Home". Leah kept telling reporters that "pressure was privilege" and she was ready to lead her team to glory.

England made it all the way to the final against Germany at Wembley. A record crowd would be cheering Leah and her team all the way to the finish line.

Leah stood in the tunnel with the captain's armband around her arm, and prepared to lead out her team. She was nervous but she was ready. There were 87,000 people dotted around the stadium but they all looked like ants.

Leah sang the national anthem with her teammates by her side, but the nerves filled her stomach. It was the biggest game of her life.

It was a tense match. England took the lead before Germany fought back, sending the game into extra time. Leah was very worried that the game was going to go to a penalty shoot-out, which is definitely one of the scariest things a professional footballer can face. However, late in extra time Chloe Kelly scored the winning goal that would finally bring home a trophy to English football after a very long wait.

England had to hold on for the last few minutes before the celebrations could begin. Leah needed to make sure the team kept focused and didn't make any mistakes. Every player battled and defended like it was the last game they would ever play. Everything Leah had learnt from playing with the boys, – the determination, the leadership, the bravery – was all coming out in this moment.

Finally, the whistle blew and Leah realized she had achieved something beyond her wildest dreams. She had led the Lionesses to glory for the very first time, in her first tournament as captain at home at Wembley. Dreams don't get much better than that.

Before celebrating with her teammates, Leah knew she had to go and do what any good captain does, go and shake hands with the opposition. Sportsmanship is very important when you're a captain. It's all about respecting the opponent and being fair, whether you win or lose. Leah went over and comforted the heartbroken German players who had fought so hard in the final.

After shaking hands with the players, she

finally got to do what she never thought would be possible when she was a little girl: lift a trophy at Wembley. With a beaming smile on her face and a skip in her step, Leah lifted the trophy with her teammates right behind her. The confetti fell down around her and the fireworks blasted in the distance. Everything was sparkling.

She had done it: a dream that was never possible to her as a little girl, and so many of the Lionesses that had come before her, was finally a reality.

⚽ ⚽ ⚽

FOOTBALL FIGURES

The UEFA Women's Euro 2022

- Seventeen million people watched England beat Germany in the final on BBC One, a record for a women's football match on TV. It was one of the most watched TV programmes of 2022.
- The tournament was watched by over 365 million people around the world.
- The final at Wembley set a record for the most attended men's or women's Euros game, with 87,192 going to the match.
- The 2022 Euros was the best attended Women's Euros of all time as a total of 574,875 went to matches across the month.
- Keira Walsh was player of the match in the final.
- Beth Mead won the golden boot prize for scoring the most goals and was also named player of the tournament.
- Mary Earps was named as the best goalkeeper.
- Alessia Russo's goal was the goal of the tournament.

LIONESSES ON THE BALL

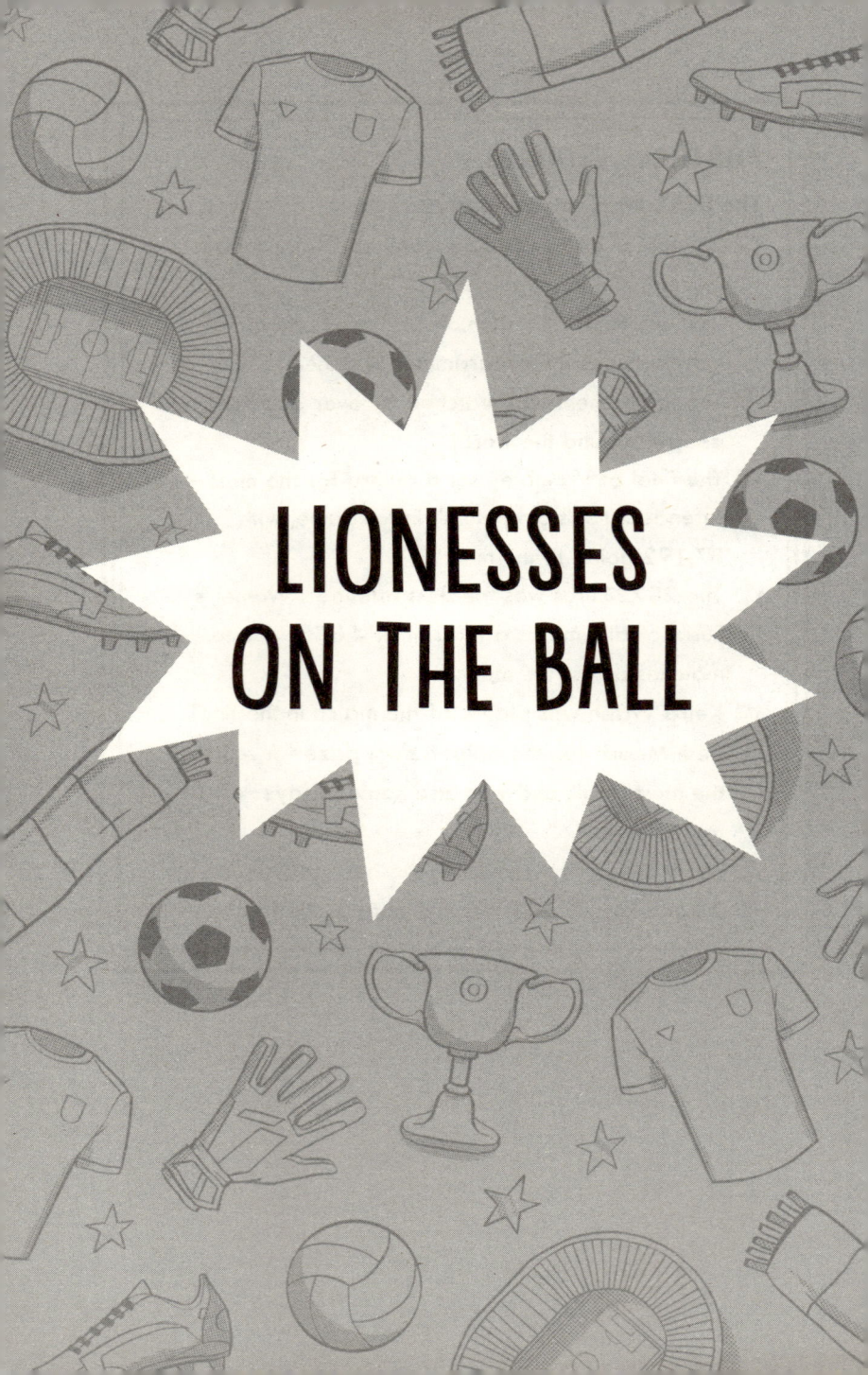

ENGLAND DEFEAT WORLD CHAMPIONS: 2022 ENGLAND VERSUS THE USA FRIENDLY

Once England won the 2022 Euros, all eyes were on them. They finally had a major trophy and would now be seen as one of the best teams in the world. They would need to consistently keep beating big teams if they were going to be seen as serious contenders for the 2023 World Cup, which is being held in Australia and New Zealand.

The next test for England after the Euros would be a friendly against the current world champions the USA in the autumn of 2022. No other team have been more successful than the Americans. They had set the standard for women's football around the world and their success had driven other nations to invest in women's football and support women's footballers.

The USA has always had the upper hand on England, losing only four times out of eighteen games. The Lionesses hadn't won since a friendly in 2017. It was going to be a massive challenge. But once again, the Lionesses had their fans behind them.

The game was a friendly at Wembley and it would be a homecoming for the Euros champions. Tickets to the game sold out in a flash. Fans waited hours on the England website trying to get them – it was like trying to get tickets to watch a famous pop star. Everyone wanted to watch the European champions take on the world champions.

The game was three months after England's Euros win but the team were still in good form and together as a group. However, a few key players had been injured in club matches since the WSL restarted.

England would be without captain Leah Williamson, an important leader for their team, and Alessia Russo, who had scored the amazing backheel in England's Euros semi-final win. But the Lionesses still had the core group who had been through all the highs and lows of the Euros. And some of the squad were playing the best football of their careers.

England knew a big challenge awaited them, but they headed into the match full of confidence. England would be taking on some huge names like Megan Rapinoe, Rose Lavelle, Crystal Dunn and exciting up and coming players Trinity Rodman and Sophia Smith.

In the week leading up to the match, all the media were talking about was the clash of two powerhouses in women's football. There were interviews with all the big names and posters all around Wembley.

Once England got to the stadium in their bus, they could already feel the excitement. There were fans everywhere, England shirts and flags lined the famous route commonly known as Wembley Way. As the team warmed up, they could hear the noise building in the stadium. The music was blasting and fans were cheering. The USA's fans had travelled a long way to come and watch the match, so the atmosphere was electric.

The match had even more significance because

in the lead up to the game, a report was released in the USA about abuse players had suffered for years in the top American league. Coaches and administrators were accused of abusing players and covering up allegations in order to protect powerful individuals rather than the players. It had been a difficult week for the team, as some had spoken up about abuse and many were friends with those who had experienced abuse.

The game was going to be a moment where players representing England and the USA could unite and show support for the victims and speaking out. The two teams walked out side by side to a huge roar. Once the national anthems had been sung, they gathered in the middle of the pitch holding a banner saying "Protect The Players". It was a powerful moment. All the fans clapped and showed their support. Then it was time for the match to begin.

England were so confident. It was completely different to when the two teams had met at the World Cup semi-final in 2019. The USA bossed that match and used their experience to grind out the win.

This time, England were the ones to tap into a champion's mindset, getting off to a brilliant start. Within ten minutes they had the lead, Lauren Hemp sticking away a ball that the USA didn't clear. England knew it wasn't going to be that easy and the USA forced goalkeeper Mary Earps to make a really good save not long after Lauren had given them the lead. England would need to be so focused to get the win and make it through this match.

But like world champions do, the USA got back into the game 20 minutes later. England had a goal kick and Mary Earps played it to Millie Bright who found Georgia Stanway on the edge of England's box. Georgia took control of the ball but she had a USA player right behind her. She could feel the pressure behind her. She tried to get out of trouble but she lost the ball and it fell to USA striker Sophia who finished past Mary and tied the game at 1–1.

Georgia was disappointed and angry with herself. She was good at getting out of positions like that, but knew against a team like the USA there wasn't time. Georgia wanted to put it right and she got her chance about five minutes later.

England won a penalty after Lucy Bronze got a boot to the head in the box. Georgia had a very good penalty record: she was one of England's best.

Georgia was handed the ball and she stepped up to the spot to take it. Alyssa Naeher, the USA goalkeeper, had saved a penalty from Steph Houghton in that 2019 semi-final, and this was a big moment for England to prove that wasn't still haunting them.

Georgia took a breath and composed herself. Once she was ready, she took a quick sprint up to the ball and struck it home with her right foot and got as much power on the ball as possible. She sent it to the bottom right-hand corner and the goalkeeper couldn't save it.

It was still only the first half and England had a lot of work to do to try and hold on to a big win. There were some uneasy moments as the referee had to intervene and use the VAR after Trinity scored an equalizer for the USA, but the goal was eventually ruled out. England somehow managed to weather the storm and hold out for a 2–1 win. It was only a friendly match, but it had been full of tension and drama and the win felt like so much more.

It wasn't the finest performance from the Lionesses and not as comfortable or convincing as their Euros wins, but England had laid down a marker. In front of a huge crowd at Wembley and against the World Champions, the Lionesses showed that they were ready to prove themselves as one of the best in the world. The scene was now set for the 2023 World Cup where the Lionesses had everything to play for.

⚽ ⚽ ⚽

THE FIFA WOMEN'S WORLD CUP 2023: KEY LIONESSES AND THEIR OPPONENTS

The FIFA Women's World Cup 2023 is being staged in Australia and New Zealand and is set to be the biggest and best women's tournament in history. It will be an exciting tournament of firsts for lots of countries:

- ⚽ For the first time, the competition will have 32 teams taking part, up from 24 in 2019.
- ⚽ It's the first time Morocco, the Philippines, the Republic of Ireland, Vietnam and Zambia will be competing in a Women's World Cup.
- ⚽ It's the first time Oceania will host a senior football tournament. It's also the first Women's World Cup to be happening in the southern hemisphere.

The prize money will also be the highest it's ever been, as it's doubled to US$60 million. It is still significantly less than the amount for the men's World Cup, which was US$440 million in 2022.

The USA head into the World Cup as the title holders after they won the 2019 edition, which was their fourth World Cup title. A lot has changed since the last tournament. The USA are still a very good team, but Europe has become a powerhouse for women's football and its teams have gone from strength to strength. Spain, Sweden, Germany and of course, England, winners of the 2022 Euros, will all be hoping to become champions. Host team Australia will also want to do well on home soil, as will reigning Olympic champions Canada. But as many teams have learnt over the years, you can never rule out the USA.

All the action will be taking place from 20 July to 20 August 2023 and I'm going to be watching every moment. I hope you enjoy the tournament too and here are the players I haven't already talked about who I think you should keep an eye on.

LIONESSES: ONES TO WATCH

⚽ MILLIE BRIGHT

Team: England
DOB: 21/08/1993
Position: Defender
Super skill: Tenacious tackling

Millie is now one of the most experienced defenders in the England team. She's powerful and known for putting her body on the line and giving everything for her team. At Chelsea, she's won nearly everything and now she's a Euros champion with England too. She's not only become one of England's most important players, she's also becoming a secret weapon in attack too, adding goals to her game.

⚽ MARY EARPS

Team: England
DOB: 07/03/1993
Position: Goalkeeper
Super skill: Shot stopper

Mary is an excellent goalkeeper for Manchester United and the England team. She's the ultimate goalkeeping genius and is very brave. Mary started her career at Leicester City and worked her way up with her goalkeeping prowess. She was a vital part of the winning squad during the 2022 Euros, playing every minute of all six games of the tournament.

⚽ ALEX GREENWOOD

Team: England
DOB: 07/09/1993
Position: Left-back, centre-back
Super skill: Set-piece specialist

Alex is mainly a left-back but can also play as a centre-back and is considered to be a set-piece specialist, meaning she's great at penalties and corners. She plays for Manchester City as well as the England team. She's very experienced and a great leader on and off the pitch.

⚽ LAUREN HEMP

Team: England
DOB: 07/08/2000
Position: Winger
Super skill: Super speed

Lauren plays for Manchester City and England. She's been a top talent ever since she was young and has grown into one of the trickiest wingers in English football. Lauren has picked up many awards and has been named as one of the best young players in the WSL multiple times. She's been a key part of Manchester City's team and is an exciting player for the future.

⚽ FRAN KIRBY

Team: England
DOB: 29/06/1993
Position: Forward
Super skill: Sensational shooting

Fran is an attacking genius for England and Chelsea. She often plays in the number 10 position, behind the striker, and is always an important creative player for her team. She can read the game like nobody else and pick out even the most difficult of passes. She has precision finishing and has done it on the big stage at World Cups, Euros and FA Cup finals at Wembley.

⚽ LAUREN JAMES

Team: England
DOB: 29/09/2001
Position: Forward
Super skill: Fearless forward

Lauren is a talented forward for Chelsea and she runs with the ball like it's stuck to her feet with glue. Football is in Lauren's blood. Her brother Reece is one of the best defenders in the world and she is one of the brightest young attacking talents. Both Lauren and her brother have become stars for Chelsea and England. When Lauren takes on a defender she always comes out on top. She has a fearless attitude and powerful finish.

⚽ ELLA TOONE

Team: England
DOB: 02/09/1999
Position: Forward
Super skill: High pressure scoring

Ella is a confident and tenacious forward and was a key part of England's 2022 Euros success, scoring in the final. Ella plays well beyond her years and is born for the big stage. With the world watching, she lobbed England into the lead at Wembley in the Euros final against Germany and she also scored the crucial goal that kept England in the quarter-final against Spain.

⚽ KEIRA WALSH

Team: England
DOB: 08/04/1997
Position: Midfielder
Super skill: Passing prowess

Keira plays as a midfielder for Barcelona and England. She is one of the most accurate passers in the game and can strike powerfully from a distance. She was part of the England team that won the UEFA Women's Euro 2022, and was named player of the match in the final.

INTERNATIONAL PLAYERS: ONES TO WATCH

⚽ ADA HEGERBERG

Team: Norway
DOB: 10/07/1995
Position: Striker
Super skill: Comeback queen

Ada embodies the Viking spirit of Norway. She's had to battle multiple injuries and fought to keep her place at the top of the game. Ada is one of the most prolific scorers in the women's game. Her stats are unbelievable and she's won pretty much everything with her club Lyon. She's smashed away hat tricks in Champions League finals and defied all the doubters to claim football's top prize the Ballon d'Or.

⚽ MANA IWABUCHI

Team: Japan
DOB: 18/03/1993
Position: Midfielder
Super skill: Close control

Mana might be small in stature but she's got a mighty heart and an incredible finish too. She's a Japanese maestro who can make things happen on the pitch. Composed, strong and skilful, Mana is a legend in her home country and in Europe where she's played on the biggest stage in the Champions League.

⚽ MARIE-ANTOINETTE KATOTO

Team: France
DOB: 01/11/1998
Position: Forward
Super skill: Slick striker

Marie-Antoinette is on the comeback trail after injuring herself at the 2022 Euros. She's determined to be stronger than ever. Up until then she had been taking Europe storm, totting up records for club and country. She has scored the most goals for Paris Saint-Germain in the club's history and is a key part of the French national team too. She's ready to take the stage at the 2023 World Cup.

⚽ SAM KERR

Team: Australia
DOB: 10/09/1993
Position: Forward
Super skill: Endless energy

Laid-back Aussie Sam is one of the biggest stars in the women's game. The super striker holds goal-scoring records all around the world, including for her national team Australia, also known as "The Matildas". Sam will be playing at home at this World Cup but that won't be tricky for her, as she was born for the big stage. The back-flipping forward loves a showpiece goal, whether it's a header, volley or something even more spectacular, she can do it all.

⚽ MARTA

Team: Brazil
DOB: 19/02/1986
Position: Forward
Super skill: Talented trickster

Marta is the brilliant footballer who has been compared to the Brazilian great Pelé. She holds the record for the most goals scored at any World Cup (17). She is considered one of the best women's footballers of all time and has won the FIFA World Player of the Year six times.

⚽ VIVIANNE MIEDEMA

Team: The Netherlands **Position:** Forward
DOB: 01/11/1998 **Super skill:** Galactic goal scorer

Vivianne has been a star ever since she was young. She made her debut for the Netherlands at just seventeen years old and hasn't looked back since. Vivianne has taken club and international football by storm and become one of the best strikers in the world. She's scored over 100 goals for Arsenal and holds the goal-scoring record for the Netherlands too.

⚽ ALEX MORGAN

Team: The USA **Position:** Striker
DOB: 02/07/1989 **Super skill:** Fantastic finishing

Alex has become a global women's football icon. She is one of the most well-known names in football and has been an elite striker for a very long time. Alex has won the World Cup twice and is an Olympic gold-medallist too. She not only managed to become one of the best in the world, but she came back as an even better player after giving birth to her daughter Charlie, challenging the idea of what it means to be a mum and a professional athlete.

⚽ ALEXANDRA POPP

Team: Germany **Position:** Striker
DOB: 06/04/1991 **Super skill:** Amazing all-rounder

Powerful Alexandra has battled lots of injuries in her career to become one of the greatest players in the world. Her impressive all-round game makes her difficult to defend against. She has trickery, finishing and is a huge threat in the air from corners and free kicks.

⚽ ALEXIA PUTELLAS

Team: Spain
DOB: 04/02/1994
Position: Midfielder
Super skill: GOAT (Greatest of All Time)

Alexia is a Spanish dynamo. She's a complete midfielder who has been voted as the best player in the world on back-to-back occasions. She has unbelievable vision, sees everything on the pitch, and can pick out the perfect pass, combining it with her lethal finish. She's a Barcelona girl through and through and has spent her whole career with the club. She missed the 2022 Euros after picking up a serious knee injury, but she's going to be back and better for 2023.

⚽ MEGAN RAPINOE

Team: The USA
DOB: 05/07/1985
Position: Midfielder, winger
Super skill: Amazing activist

Megan is way more than just a footballer, she's an activist and a campaigner. She combines her showstopping and championship-winning performances on the pitch as an attacking midfielder with selfless activist work. She has campaigned against racism, gender equality and for the rights of LGBTQ+ people around the world. She's a two-time World Cup winner and Olympic champion and loves to express herself through bright hair and loud clothes.

⚽ WENDIE RENARD

Team: France
DOB: 20/07/1990
Position: Centre-back
Super skill: Defending dynamo

Wendie is the defensive giant who, at six foot two inches (1.88 metres), has been a brick wall for France and Lyon for over a decade. She's a tough tackler and an important leader for club and country. She's won it all with Lyon but is still waiting to claim a big trophy with France.

⚽ KHADIJA "BUNNY" SHAW

Team: Jamaica
DOB: 31/01/1997
Position: Forward
Super skill: Unstoppable power

Bunny is one of the greatest players Jamaica has ever produced. She's a national hero and quickly becoming one of the most threatening strikers in the game. Bunny is strong in the air, physical and tall. She can put so much power in a header but also apply the softest of touches for a smooth finish. She will carry Jamaica's hopes on her shoulders at the World Cup, but it's a pressure she relishes.

FLO LLOYD-HUGHES is a football journalist and broadcaster. She has written for the *Guardian* and *The Athletic*, and is a regular on the podcast "Wrighty's House" with Ian Wright. Flo is also host of the women's football podcast "Counter Pressed" on Spotify. Flo has been covering the men's and women's game for the last eight years: writing, broadcasting, directing and producing content for the BBC, Sky Sports and talkSport. *The Rise of the Lionesses* is her first book.